Contents

Vol 93 No 3 Aut

Poems

Essays

Reviews

Poet in the Gallery

Art

Poems

Tony Lopez

IN PHOTOGRAPHS

A pair of Iranian twins joined at the head
far from settling this increasingly bitter row
swiftly and grimly appeared to transmit the story
because it had been in the public interest
an inquiry into the good faith of one man
from Hereford to London misrepresented the situation
when an express train hit a transit van
the politics was driving the intelligence
when an express train hit a transit van
let me tell you how the scores have changed
possibly pronounced "STROOD" as far as I know
three people, believed to be fruit pickers, died
and may have been acting in good faith
although we were divided on that issue but otherwise
supporters of the gay priest now not-to-be Bishop of Reading
Iraqis provide information about attacks on Americans
the veracity and honesty of our government
I wondered whether that was worth saying
whether or not the claim was well grounded, well founded, I mean
either a cow or a woman with a cow's horns
became prime minister in 1958 and was assassinated
back in apartheid days
Mr Straw calls for an apology from the BBC
let me tell you how the scores have changed
fourteen to Mr Good
this long-range ballistic missile travels 800 miles
without seeing the actual documents
about whom we know nothing
nor do we know his motive on the basis of evidence
whether there was undue pressure
and where exactly is Kim Bauer now?
if the claim was not well founded
chemical or biological weapons could be launched
whether politics was driving the intelligence
which he had typed up on a very long roll of paper
taken from the foreign affairs select committee

in a transit van: a clear and present threat
needed to be established or not
and the evidence was to the contrary
that the 45 minute claim
could have been avoided
and the people were misled and the parliament was misled
denied access to witnesses
about whom we know nothing
and Jack Straw hangs by his thumbs then passes out
tries to pull the rip-cord but passes out
is shocked by a security man rogue element
falling on a dodgy dossier, he passes out
he looks worn out but handsome in Arab dress
they hang him up again by the thumbs
and he is interrogated by Robin Cook
who wants to know about allegations made
by a gay priest from Reading called Elizabeth Bishop
whether politics was driving the intelligence
making this 45 minute speech
or whether it was in fact a sky-dive
a man addicted to risk
making a complete *Horlicks*
falling out of the sky
but acting in good faith
like a certain celibate not-to-be Bishop
serving on the joint intelligence committee
and not the other way around
Mr Bauer called for an apology between 2AM and 3AM
when the bomb went off in the desert
as far as possible from Los Angeles: maybe Phoenix
maybe Tucson, maybe Basra, maybe Janin
the verdict NOT PROVEN
I wondered whether it was worth saying
whether or not the claim was well founded
how much it would cost to get a bulldozer
how much should I allow on the arts council application form?
what would be the appropriate delivery system
to get it over the level crossing
and into the settlements in good faith?

Kate Clanchy

ON BREAST-FEEDING,

of which I am strongly in favour,
in the same way as when I visited China
and walked down the Ceremonial Road
where formerly only the Emperor
(or Emperor and Procession: eunuchs,
closed litters of chrysanthemum silk)
walked once a year on the winter solstice,
past the shut shutters and frozen hush
of the entire interdicted populace; when I,
on a merely touristic visit, walked
this sacred road to the Round Altar
of the Temple of Heaven (which is round
in itself, the Temple, round after round
of glazed blue roof ascending) when I
clambered up the glittering tiers of the three
concentric alabaster terraces and stood
at the top in the innermost circle, on the spot
which once held the Throne of Heaven,
which marked the centre of everything,
the very middle of the Middle
(or should we say Central?) Kingdom,
when I did this not alone, but with crowds,
with Chinese in their hundreds, with
tour groups, students and families all
laughing, all joshing, all testing the echoes,
all posing for photos, everywhere
but above all on that central spot, on
the site where, for five centuries, only
the Emperor had ever stood (the Emperor,
tasting the dust of the solstice, observing
the ranks of silent silk rumps), when
I saw instead people dashing to beat

the self-timer, families in nuclear
and extended formations, troupes
in uniforms, miniskirts, yellow tour teeshirts,
in apparently ironic Mao badges and caps –

I was strongly in favour of that.

REJOICE IN THE LAMB

At night, in your shift, fine hair upright
you are my tiny Bedlamite,
admonishing the laughing crowd
with your pale, majesterial hands,
or roaring out like poor Kit Smart
how blessed, electric, all things are.

LOVE

I hadn't met his kind before.
His misericord face – really,
like a joke on his father – blurred
as if from years of polish;
his hands like curled dry leaves;

the profligate heat he gave
out, gave out, his shallow,
careful breaths: I thought
his filaments would blow,
I thought he was an emperor,

dying on silk cushions.
I didn't know how to keep
him wrapped, I didn't know
how to give him suck, I had
no idea about him. At night

I tried to remember the feel
of his head on my neck, the skull
small as a cat's, the soft spot
hot as a smelted coin,
and the hair, the down, fine

as the innermost, vellum layer
of some rare snowcreature's
aureole of fur, if you could meet
such a beast, if you could
get so near. I started there.

Anthony Caleshu

IN IRELAND, AFTER THE LEGALIZATION OF DIVORCE

Where there is a concern for tightness the water rushes
like breath over stone, and I am tired of explaining myself
through the brush. Short legs dangling, I sit like the Sphinx
on this stone foot bridge, asking riddles of longevity
every time you cross, trying to move me to resume our walk.
Hear me, O Love, I say, with the voice of the entire
Catholic church behind me: where once the blue skies of God
used to meet in our grass stained backs,
there is soon to be only the barrenness of space and rock,
rock and hard space – no longer the need for vegetation as cushion.
But the Catholic voice is a tough one to emulate
and mine breaks like the dark sky soon will.

*

My hands cupped full with wants,
you answer with your hips, because they too are anxious
as the leaves are to fall. Against this tree with you,
explicitly, I want never to stand on my own toes.
You move over me like a river over beds of moss-covered slate.
I look behind you to see a pack of wild dogs, whimpering desertion,
eating green grass. You are right to see rain in the dogs' jowls.
And with the downpour, we rush into an old barn
that tells the story of an old barn, where each September
I gather, and you come. The stove heats a corner,
and our love heats the stove that cooks our morning fry.
We eat with no shortness of breath. We are full in the lungs
and loose with one another as runny eggs – the yolks sunny side up –
the rashers blackened like we like them.
We leave with no questions answered and fewer questions asked.
We huddle through the winter into cakes of soap.
We scrub one another warm and raw.

Jeremy Reed

NARCISSUS

It's the poached egg co-ordinates,
orange eye in a ruffle
of ivory frills

and the scent of a sharp Pouilly Fume
klatchy in Hyde Park borders,
reactivates Martyn's last spring

and a macaroon of cherry blossom
bitty outside like pink snow
dusting each hospital visit,

St. Mary's alien as a moon hotel
in Paddington, its AIDS ward stashed
with carriers top of a viral count

nuking the brain's blood barrier.
He wore a mink over cashmere,
and picked at tarte au citron

we scooped from a patisserie catwalk
efflorescent as Philip Treacy –
all glazed fruit saucers in lace doilies.

His pill-take was 40 a day,
an apocalyptic chemical offensive.
I'd walk back through the park root-chilled,

observing maroon foot wells
sunk like black eyes in cherry blossom.
Narcissi were grouped like Socratic

epigoni, instructed by the myth
of dying into an image
conceived as fatal attraction.

Today I review their regenerative
uptake in April, my memories
hurting like six years of snow exposure.

Robert Stein

HOMO

And here is the man whom we should remember,
Half a day from Joppa and lost by the sea.
His tongue is dust, arms casually broken.
No kings, no lilies, no blood, no tree.

Mario Petrucci

BREATHING

Chernobyl 1986

They had to teach me
from scratch. Teach me

    to breathe. As though
    I had fallen out of space or

up from water and breath
was labour – each breath

    a pang to draw me back
    from the brink. In. Out. In

this world life is indifferent.
You must will it in. Will it

    out. I look at my son –
    those white cheeks that

tight frown and
I wonder how I can

    breathe. He says – *Mama*
    when you go to sleep to-

night please don't forget to
breathe. Please. He is

    not allowed to run. Or
    jump. Like that boy who

hanged himself with a
belt. I watch him. And he

       watches me – when I doze
       on the red sofa he rests a

hand to check the rise and
fall of my chest. Tells me he

       will teach me in his dreams –
       will teach me to breathe if

I teach him how to fly. *If*
you go with Grandpa he

       says – *will you be able to*
       breathe? He says this and

his cheeks run wet and
he runs short of breath so

       we sit once again to
       teach each other how —

deep and slow. *We are*
flying I tell him. *We are*

       breathing   he replies.

Carrie Etter

LAND-LOCK

If we are winged, they falter before us.
There is no suppressing the song, and disavowal angers them.
On Mondays they resemble young children
on the first day of school, they follow
with affectionate interest, most gazing openly
while a few extend a hand to feel the outermost feathers.
By Thursdays, however, they snigger like men long out of work,
they grumble over backgammon and leave no opening at the table.
On Fridays they try to ply us with drink, while on Saturdays,
on Sundays, they neither distinguish us from the crowd
nor greet us with cheer. On Mondays the palimpsest looks bare again,
though faint traces remain to warrant our wariness.

If they are winged, we imagine their homes aflame
and warm our hands at the conflagration.
There is no denying the music, and its absence can cause agony.
On Mondays they could be our first teachers,
their gracious smiles bestow a sense of boundlessness
that proves our greatest, perhaps purest pleasure.
On Wednesdays their frowns are legendary, which makes their attempts
to join us, on Thursdays, no small matter for indignation.
On Fridays, nevertheless, we give them a glass in the payday ease
with which we lavish drink among ourselves, while on Saturdays,
on Sundays, the seized reprieve lasts long enough
that on Mondays we easily return their gentleness.

The prairie spills in every direction until night
circumscribes the town, releases its burden of stars.

THE TABOO

Under the cover of others' indifference, I yank the flag from its post and carry it from the lush meadow to a desolate stretch of bare earth, from its territorial declaration to its impotence. I expected, when I stepped out of the grass, for the flag's weight to lessen as its symbolism fell away. Kicking, stomping, defacing with sprays of dirt, no act relieved me of its imposition. There was only one thing to do. I restored it to its former stance, not, as we say, good as new, for a smear persisted in its folds, but now it was back, aloft, waving, where I could hate it with reverence.

A. C. Bevan

AN APOLOGY FOR POETRY

i have taken
the words
that were on
the icebox

& which
you were probably
saving
for sestinas

forgive me
they were magnetic
so
    sweat

& so
    could

Andrew Sant

TWO WAYS OF LOOKING AT LANDSCAPE

1

(China)

Not for us Li Bai's sublime moon, his uplifted eyes;
the terrain is steep, and Chinese herbs
I'm shown are prepared to save us, by degrees,

from sore feet and vertiginous thoughts.
Put a lyric in the pot and it would produce steam.
We take each step wisely and, later, tea.

2

(Sweden)

Two of us here with words to share. This northern landscape
echoes them: fir, *furn*; birch, *bjork*; lily, *lilje*.
The *snegle* I nearly crush, and the *orm*.

Up ahead our related words are gathered, damp, darkening,
till we'll not notice the forest for the words.
They'll be the light we guess by. We'll see.

Yvonne Green

THERE IS A BOAT

There is a boat I've seen before
I've sailed in it or been told
of dark disabled seas which rend
the clothes and hook the conscious
which take the walking in the square
with handles of a bag crossed
one girl holding each and feeling
the scratch of a struggling hen
on the pink of her legs on the
spirit of her tender years laughing
laughing for years into the future
girls again that day they took
the hen to the slaughter with never
a description of the journey home
the bag must have been heavier
and there would have been a different smell

There's crew on the boat
crew in whites and nods
my plate is decorated
with fish bones and parsley
the sea spray the sea speaking
what we know and we make no move
confused our crew look different now
not ashamed still crisp their arms
still busied relieved of the excuse

A boy walks naked
with the sun and his salopettes
reminding him of his skin
his feet feeling the grasses
on soles as pink as a puppy's
his lips smoking a hard reed
rolling it saving its suck

I know you will say
that we saw and took action
and that we saw nothing
but the white of uniforms
pressed or that we and they
stepped forward and backward
and sat down and stood up
cried laughed ran waited
caused it didn't deserve it
were powerful had no influence
were victims were perpetrators
lived among you were never seen
took were too visible integrated
legitimated illegitimated
were the object of envy admiration
disgust confusion

The wind vomits up black spray
and stings my arms where the fine hairs
grow black in large follicles
I'm eating salt without noticing
but my forearms notice
the sea turns red and this time
I look for words

Angela Leighton

FLYING WESTWARDS: 2 OCTOBER 2002

Feast of All Angels that fly by day,
by daylight's lightweights, cirrus-floored,
a white lagging in the world's roofspace,
and soul, a microlite or boeing,
nosing through a blue bend,
tilting a shoulder-bladed wing
to weightlessness, no-holds, some going's
sheer precarious openness and cold.

Imagine an angel come to light.
Its glass skin adjusts sunshine
to intravenous blue. It is exacting,
full also, as angels are,
of the bright capacity of nothing.

Light-headed light, a lens reversed,
our watch stopwatched, not clockwise wise,
the soul's acrostic lost in sky's
round trip, pure optical hasard,
stinting the minutes we mark, then hours –
sun and wing like God and Adam,
in the beginning.

A sweepstake blue takes all we are,
eyebright, cup of unconsummated summer,
sun-trap, unendurable verandah –
sky letting
whatever warmth the earth breathes, out,
making light,
in the turned jar's almost-nowhere,
of what we were, love, under the heavens above.

Richard Lambert

THOMPSON AND THOMSON

Will they come, those sombre gentlemen,
with black suits, and ties,
and soft looks to the corner of the garden
as if to avoid the issue or find a flower,

the gentlemen with rolled umbrellas,
twirling their moustaches,
whose murmured conversations
may never be overheard,

will they come,
with notebooks from their inside pockets and serious expressions,
and hang an umbrella upon an arm
while they wet the end of their pencil, then scribble?

BRACELET

And all the geese that fly
from here to God knows where
are only ways to tell all will be well,
like the plastic bracelet the newborn wears
or the goose, or where first finger and thumb touch.

Dawn Wood

TO A MAN CAST IN A HARD ROLE

The end, when it happens, will be local,
perhaps in a year or so. Meantime,
my advice would be to sing –

sing as if you have stumbled
into a sweet, stone cathedral,
as if to lift the pigeons with you from the greasy steps;

those diamond notes could stir
the founder's marble foot,
could score a plate-glass dove through stains.

Stand on your bones, breathe with the building.
The end, when it happens,
will have you stifling laughter –

you and the others –
biting mouth ulcers, still unable to contain it.
Then, give in.

IMAGINING A PALESTINIAN SUNBIRD DRINKING LILAC

So much nectar
        you could swim in it
or it in you

you could assimilate
a sugar flux
spin a sun-drop into a net

conduct
        exchange
                conduct

you could   hold
                 spill
                 hum

isn't that she
coming to me
nearly here

Brian Fewster

ONE STEP AT A TIME

You had no hall. Behind the door
of your front room the letters lay
like drifts of decomposing leaves.
You stepped across them twice a day.

You stepped across them twice a day
while junk promotion, final bill
and family tidings cried at you.
The cries ascended small and shrill.

The cries ascended small and shrill
of courts, of creditors to pay.
With steadfastness like Saint Jerome
you turned your conscious mind away.

You turned your conscious mind away,
but some disturbance stirred there still.
A breasting wave blocked out your light.
A shadow paralysed your will.

A shadow paralysed your will.
You turned your conscious mind away.
The cries ascended small and shrill.
You stepped across them twice a day.

Michael Symmons Roberts

THE CLOTHES

Back late, I leave a slumped
self-portrait on the chair,
a splayed corpse, limbs akimbo.

If I believed the soul
was separate from the body,
I might describe myself

as the soul of my clothes,
cut loose in an unlit afterlife
beneath a massive canopy of night.

My threads are guardians,
vigil-keepers at the bedside,
sleeping on the job.

In the half-light, they show
me hopelessly drunk, shot
through the heart, or drowned.

They are my boneless likeness,
a lightning conductor,
decoy for bad dreams.

E. A. Markham

GOD OF THE FLAT

You go back to those days when the debate
made less sense, when you were privileged
to live in a large house, and one duty,
they said, to outthink the undeserving,
was to construct a god big as the house.
And we tried over the years for a twelve-
roomed god, clever enough to stand all night
at the front and back yards and on those bits

of land worked by folk whose gods were too small
to travel. Fruit-trees in the garden, pigs
and chickens had their gods. Then we were safe
till the logic hit us that friends who lived
in more-roomed houses would despise the size
of our god, and we fled the scene in shame.

AN ACT IN THE COMEDY

The eye gives out
In the middle of my book
As if to deny a fond destiny

For reading and writing.
So the joke stops
At this latest indignity.

The way back from the dentist
Through the university park
Is risky in the holiday season.

A heart-attack here
Where no one might come
For days, cannot be made funny.

So take the public path
Where some passing reveller
Might pause in the spirit

Of the occasion.
And put the boot in
And put the boot in.

No lighter reading, this,
But chances are you'll go out
With *some* ceremony.

Hamish Ironside

SEROXAT®

I'll be sensible, I lied. Then it came true.
As warm as summer bricks: my secret hobby.
It reaches through my body like a tree.
In ten to fourteen days I'm feeling happy
to settle for what others settle for.
Now sleepless nights are pleasant anti-climax;
the girls are sport, the thrill gone with the fear.
The time will come to pass through other climates.

Inside the book beneath the pillow: *fraud.*
Was that before or this behind that rote?
The cross you cross not waking up afraid.
The language problem but you have to write.
They moved the tree and told us it was freed.
Suppose to lop the branch they cut the root?

Simon Barraclough
SEROXAT®

Monday to Sunday, calendar-packed,
blister-wrapped, stepping stones across
a tinfoil plain that would jag
like metal on filling were it not
for these chalky Sherpas,
ushering me from and to my bed.
These are my morning-after, evening-before,
afternoon-during pills.

My parents led me deep into the forest,
so I shed a trail of white pellets,
only for birds to snaffle them up
and leave me stranded. But they fell
from the sky as a thudding black rain.
I followed the broken birds home again.

Linda Chase

CELLAR DANCE

'A man dancing naked in the cellar'
is not a story to dine out on.
It is just one of the secrets of the house
kept in the dark, next to the laundry room,
though lots of people saw him.

I mean he had music, for Christ's sake
and rows of benches for the audience.

It was no accident, no chance event,
not something I stumbled on in the dark
without being led to the witness seat
by a young man with a torch
who invited me to sit down and I did.

I could have teased you, made a story
of the gradual unfolding – for instance,
how I first saw his shoulder
with the tiniest bit of light behind it
and I could see he was not wearing a shirt.
He was sitting behind a big box
which let only his upper torso show.
I didn't give the rest of his body a thought.

Not until he stood up, holding a tiny red light
in each of his hands.
No. Light is too strong a word –

just parts of the dark
which were no longer black,
but had turned red instead.

He danced with his arms in the air
like a brand new bear in the forest,
as if he knew no other creatures were looking.

Of course I looked. Everyone did –
quite hard too, forcing our eyes around the dim
edge of his body against the flaking cellar walls
to see what parts of him flounced to the music
describing a man, only a man
dancing naked in the cellar.

Tony Lopez

AFTER

some of these abstracts
totally excluded
from old romances
the level of structure

towards better translation
in rectangle 3
the self cannot find
a theoretical foothold

for peculiar delights
you square with this
a human wish
appears as a mode

whose dominant function
or working arrangement
a shift in scale
between two systems

falling back into
the carnivalesque
we witness a series
augmenting the real

to discover a pretext
or beloved scruple
when she was old
found double joy

jumping off hilltops
they slowly rise
which might be argued
in flickering time

by using a grid
the process continues
through paradigm shifts
to deliver ordnance

according to a pattern
previously determined
in sand or glass
anxiety is

without a centre
located in history
by this device
a third class road

a railway line
in one direction
almost explicit
internal repetition

fills available space
endlessly branching
unspeakable objects
uncovered in time

cut down even
across the city
home this method
an hour each day

feels soft inside
thy woodland shape
breathing black smoke
streaks fall down

a kind of therapy
leads artless troops
to find the many
dreaming of ease

but others walk
led in plain clothes
heaps pile up
moving people along

full of enemies
become suddenly dumb
a hope or dream
white coral beaches

some force of allusion
crashed in mercy
wrecked planes fall
into their appearance

the years a fraud
glow of gold
phosphorous flare
falls into the sea

to push for day
set loose the cry
blue among blue
jet trails dissolve

a cloud of snow
a last spring freak
and in the dark
echoes long after

as if even now
smoke rises into distance
spreads and moves far
while still you sleep

snow blows across ice
where gold is stored
shapes in clouds
lead into oblivion

we lived here then
beating a small drum
is almost like nothing
a rose that climbs

the people were blue
turned into smoke
flowers cut down
in public gardens

in broken glass
some years before
made up our minds
fire in the night

returns to a shell
sent out to dig
when dark comes down
they lived here then

earth is at hand
the last cloudy streak
its meaning a vapour
a figure of speech

Pierre Reverdy

THE DRY LANGUAGE

The nail is there
       Keeping at a slant
The clear shreds of breeze turning blasted
    everyone who might see
       The whole street nude
the road the pavement the view the gates are
    blinding
        Not a rain-drop
        Not a leaf from the tree
        No shade from clothes
           I'm waiting
               the railway station in the distance
The river flows on as you hike up the cutting
    earth dry as a bone
       the whole world is nude it's all bleached

With the clock ticking away to the wrong time
         the train's racket has gone
          I'm waiting

MIRACLE

Head hanging
            Lashes curly
Mouth shut
The lamps are lit
There's nothing except in a name
                        Which one forgets
When the door opens
And I daren't enter
            It's all going on behind the scenes

One talks
        I eavesdrop a little

My future hangs in the balance next door

BELL RINGING

    All lights dim
Breezes go chanting
            With trees chilly
The beasts dead
There's no one about
                        See
The stars cease to shine
            The earth never to turn again
A head shakes
            Hair sweeps away evening
The final church tower is there
            Strikes twelve

FOR HE WHO WAITS

It's great when autumn comes around
Sing someone
But no one
But me
Bothers
I'll be the last one

She's not that upset
As you said
This grey period
A morsel of melancholy
For you to give your reasons

The smoke questions
Is it him or you
Who will shout yes
Before first freezing

And me I'm waiting
The final glimmer
Which floats through the night

As the ground falls
And it's not finished yet
A wing holds it up
For an eternity
I'll walk you to the very end
To shut the door
If it's not blowing a gale

MEMORY

In a minute
            And I am returned
Of all that's happened I've retained nothing
A point
            The high heavens
                              And on the final second
The light flashes passed
                  Footsteps one hears
Everything that walks as one halts
You let it all go
            And what there is within
The lights that dance
            The shadows lengthen
Spaces multiply
            If you see the future
A prison where a real beast jumps
Chest and arms create a similar movement
A woman giggled
                  Her head tossed back
And the passer-by who arrived misplaced us
We three were never identified
But still we were there
                  Filled with expectation

FROM MY TOE-ENDS

There's nothing at rest
      between the fingers of both hands
The other which disappears
      In the middle
      the shuffling of feet
Throttle that raised voice
That which groaned and that which would not stop
That which ran too quickly
It was you stopped this passion in its tracks
      The aspiration and feeling smug
      which are gone on the breeze
The leaves are falling
      while the birds count
         the rain drops
The lights switched off behind blinds
Don't walk so quickly
With that unholy row you'll mess it all up if you're not careful

Translated by Simon Smith

Essays

The *Poetry Review* Essay

TOBY LITT

Writing

Where do you get your Inspiration from?

For the public, all writers whether of poetry or of prose are still Romantics – Shelley-come-latelys – still muse-haunted sensitives, victims of the descending, perhaps-bestowed word. Other artforms have managed to place someone or something between themselves and this version of the creation myth: classical music had Serialism, sculpture Duchamp, painting Warhol. Literature, however, despite the resolutely anti-Romantic efforts of the Dadaists, William Burroughs and the OuLiPo movement, has yet to convince either the public or, I would say, itself that it derives from anything other than Inspiration.

Perhaps the biggest reason for the continuing dominance of the Romantic account of composition is that many writers find it, in all sincerity, true to their desk-experience. There are, for such writers, undoubted advantages to letting those around them continue to believe in it. Being struck by the muse – or rather, *saying* you have been struck by the muse – is a great way of getting people to fuck off and leave you alone; even if all you really want to do is settle down with a cup of tea and the crossword. Tea and the crossword may be an important part of the creative process; walking, hoovering, getting drunk, too. But these may be harder to explain to the People from Porlock.

Writers lie to themselves consistently about how they work – about how their work works – and I doubt if I can make myself much of an exception. But I will try.

What have we seen of how writing takes place? Cinema has largely failed to represent it – the recently released *Adaptation* is the second-best ever film about writers and how they do what they do; the best, of course, is *The Shining*. Even as worthy an attempt as *Dorothy Parker and the Vicious Circle* has to resort to the cinematic cliché of –

INT. STUDY. NIGHT.
The clack-clack of typing. Close-up on a wastepaper basket, full of scrunched-up, typed-on sheets. We hear a sigh, a mutter, a curse. Scrunk – as the latest sheet is ripped

from the typewriter. We watch as it bounces, tightly scrunched, off the top of the pile, lands on the floor.

This is the best Hollywood has been able to manage. And the Indies haven't done any better.

So, where *do* I get my inspiration from? Sidestep: the history of writing is, in many departments, that of a descent. In *The Moronic Inferno*, Martin Amis traces a descent of subject: "In thumbnail terms, the original protagonists of literature were gods; later, they were demigods; later still, they were kings, generals, fabulous lovers, at once superhuman, human and all too human; eventually they turned into ordinary people… Nowadays, our protagonists are a good deal lower down the human scale than their creators: they are anti-heroes, non-heroes, sub-heroes." Similarly, the location of the source of inspiration has plunged down from God-plain-and-simple, to the God-inspired poet, to the thing-inspired poet (Nature, Woman, Beauty), to the self-inspired poet, all the way to the non-existent poet. Long before Barthes posited the death of the author, historicist critics were making the argument that *Paradise Lost* would have been written even had Milton never existed.

I don't believe this to be case, in my case; I know that if I hadn't lived in Prague I wouldn't have written three novels about Prague; I know that had I not written those novels, no-one else would have. Writers, I would argue, *are* capable, for some reason, of having an engaged relationship with the zeitgeist – a two-way relationship. I would also defend Shelley's "unacknowledged legislators" claim: had it not been for the poets of courtly love, the world would not be in thrall to another version of the Romantic. Before "cool" came along, love *über alles* was the greatest viral ideology the world had known (now it is "cool vincit omnia"; but that's another subject). The disposition of their affections is what is most important to anyone in the world who has been exposed to the idea of poetic love. This was *written*; love was a creation of writers. They took Plato's grotesque image of wheeling, four-limbed proto-humanoids, split in two and separated around the world, and they made it the felt truth. There can be no greater legislation than that of hearts.

It is easy, and fun, to give literary critics a good duffing up. Yeats, in "The Scholars", defined them as belated misunderstanders:

> Bald heads forgetful of their sins,
> Old, learned, respectable bald heads
> Edit and annotate the lines
> That young men, tossing on their beds,
> Rhymed out in love's despair
> To flatter beauty's ignorant ear.

But I would argue that critics, whilst the best readers we have of the Written, are, in general, almost useless with regards to *writing* – writing, as Frost put it, which "rides on the flux of its own melting". And this despite the fact that they, the critics, come to me, and to themselves, in the form of the written, of the being-written word. Critical writing intersects with towards-literary writing, but for the most part it avoids wildness, lostness, hopelessness (though Derrida often manages all three). Every useful insight and piece of advice I have ever read about sentence-making came from a poet, a short-story writer, or a novelist.

When the writing is going well (I am avoiding the word "inspired") it feels as if someone has taken my brain out and filled my head with a very cheap and chemical-heavy soft drink – orangeade or cherryade; I call this state "headfizz". The bubbly liquid being shaken up behind my eyes is brightly-coloured, almost day-glo (this brightness is the manifestation of a kind of internal embarrassment: I want to say to myself "fuck off and leave me alone"); I would assume, if at this moment a brainscan were to be taken, the synapses would be seen to be getting themselves in something of a lather. I remember an aside from Les Murray, after a reading at the Troubador, about how he liked to chuck the poem into the back brain, not feel it was being dictated too directly by the flippant forelobes.

I also remember Graham Swift likening his writing process to wiping the dust off an inscription, off a gravestone. Any writer putting forward this argument – that of the pre-existence of the words, their finishedness before they arrive at them – is lying. The lie may be necessary, to avoid confonting the Great Terror – the Great Terror being that the blank page is actually that, and that what they are doing is not deciphering but cobbling together. Graham Swift wishes to be like an archaeologist, perhaps even really wishes he was an archaeologist, because he can't live with the truth that he's something else, something worse, not even a graverobber: a *faker*.

The greatest single anti-Romantic aesthetic confession I've ever come across is in Edgar Allan Poe's "The Philosophy of Composition":

> Most writers – poets in especial – prefer having it understood that they compose by a species of fine frenzy – an ecstatic intuition – and would positively shudder at letting the public take a peep behind the scenes, at the elaborate and vacillating crudities of thought – at the true pur-poses seized only at the last moment – at the innumerable glimpses of the idea that arrived not at the maturity of full view – at the fully matured fancies discarded in despair as unmanageable – at the cautious selections and rejections – at the painful erasures and interpolations – in a word, at the wheels and pinions – the tackle for scene-shifting – the

> step-ladders and demon-traps – the cock's feathers, the red paint and
> the black patches, which, in ninety-nine cases out of the hundred, con-
> stitute the properties of the literary *histrio.*

The dirty secret of writing, as Poe makes permanently plain, is that bad is often a necessary step towards good. The world may see the monster but Frankenstein sees only the stitches, the bolt.

When I began to write, I was abashed by lists – I felt myself inadequate because I couldn't, straight out, write a sentence like: "There are seven reasons why blah blah blah… and here they are in descending order of importance." I believed that the creators of lists wrote them down that way, without a blot. I was deceived; I believed that the surface of the page I was reading had been, somehow, excreted in that perfected form by a real writer. I hadn't read Poe. Perhaps I even went so far as to believe that the words were a discovered inscription, and that I would never make a word-archaeologist; still, I was determined.

What I have learnt since is that, as the old saw sings, writing is rewriting; and not just rewriting of the words but of the writer. Cancellation of a line is also a minor act of self-cancellation. How do bad writers become good? Alexander Pope knew the answer: "I believe no one qualification is so likely to make a good writer, as the power of rejecting his own thoughts, and it must be this (if anything) that can give me a chance to be one."

Each present-time erasure alters in a tiny, tiny way what a writer is likely to be willing, in future, to put on paper. (It is often forgotten, particularly by literary critics, that writing is written in the present. However engraved or discovered it may look, it was at one time performed onto the page.) And so all writers write their way out of the primeval sludge and stodge of bad words with which they began, by crossing their bad selves out. A crapness deleted becomes a step, and all writers, to follow this line of argument, are on their way to being great; some just move faster than others, are quicker learners, hate their crap selves more. Writing, to define it, is a continuous process of self-criticism motivated by aesthetic self-disgust, self-hate. Hate powers. Hate is the motor force; hate of the embarrassment and humiliation and suicide-inducing idea of being an uninteresting self – of being a self unworthy of being written and incapable of being well-written.

Seen this way, writers don't *have* ideas, they *are* ideas; ongoing, ramifying – at the very least, they are the idea that they are or will one day be a writer; at the most, they are the best the language can, in their historical moment, do. (All any writer can hope to be is "the best living", the best of their period; what they then have to do is hope that their period is a great one. I will return to this.)

Writing as the performed self can best be explained by analogy with music, it is writing-as-jazz. The genius of the improvisation is dependent upon the years of hours of practice; the eight bars of God-kissing couldn't exist without the woodshed. Charlie Parker didn't play bum notes. He had good and bad nights, sessions, but never failed to be Parker. To write, really to write, is equivalent to having achieved an unmistakable tone on the piano – like Art Tatum, like Thelonius Monk – the piano, an instrument that any fool can get chopsticks out of. And this is the real question-to-be-asked. Not *Where does your inspiration come from?* but *How can you possibly be capable of forcing the language into distinctiveness?* Or, more shortly, *How did you come to own these words?* Compared to language, compared, in other words, to speech plus the dictionary plus the pile-up of all that has been written plus the speeding juggernaut of all that is being written, the piano is a cinch to personalise. Lurking behind the public idea of Inspiration is another idea: although writing is, in great part, the use of language uniquely, surely such an achievement is beyond a single person. Inspiration is a good explanation, otherwise the writer must either have cheated or have had help. Inspiration is a way of giving credit at the same time as credit is being taken away.

And I'm still, in some ways, managing to avoid answering the question: *Where does it come from?* Which, for me, is where the problems really begin – but the problems are also the project. Because although I don't believe in Barthes' unauthored texts, or that I am the inkjet printer of a particular stage of late Capitalism, I don't want merely to pick my own regression. This is the easiest way out; a self-Romanticization, leaving the writer free, like the literary critics, to concentrate on the written and not on the moment of writing. Romanticism allows the writer to be absent from their own process: the hands can touch-type whilst the eyes are looking out the window at the sunset. I don't believe, though, that the great writers of the past were ever *faux-naïf* – not about their workings, nor their work, nor their world. (I don't mean Heaney, Larkin, Carver, Frost, Hemingway, Lawrence, Hardy, Dickens; I mean Beckett, Celan, Joyce, Rilke, Proust, James, Browning, Flaubert.) They did what they did at a point of necessary awareness, and hence difficulty. And this is where the problems become the project: not that writing must self-consciously display its self-consciousness – wink too often and people take it for a tic – but that the Romantic account of composition, at the time of Wordsworth and Coleridge, was an honest attempt to articulate the means of word-production.

I would return, in order to explain "where inspiration comes from" as accurately as I can, to Poe's "Philosophy". Writing falls onto the page haphazardly, but frequently reads as seamless.

When I am teaching creative writing classes, I tend to tell the students two things: *You are forgiven* and *You can.* (The inspirational speaker tone is deliberate.) The second statement is intended to forestall delaying-tactic questions of the "If I wanted to X could I Y?" sort. There is an anecdote about the philosopher J L Austin. He was asked by the child of one of his friends whether time-travel was possible. Austin said something along the lines of, "Well, no-one's done it so far. But why don't you have a really good go, and see whether you can". A lot more will be learnt in the trying-and-failing than in the listening to reasons why not. Which feeds back into the first statement; that in the pursuit of something as ludicrous as time-travel, there is no humiliation in any kind of failure. By making the effort, honestly, you are pre-forgiven.

To write is to engage, paradoxically, in a self-critical wildness of mind; the easiest way to deal with this is mentally to separate all the wildness off into the first draft, and to leave the revision and re-revision in the well-manicured hands of the self-critic. But the two states, in my experience, interpenetrate: there is wild criticism, there is critically aware wildness. Another way to cope with the paradox is to pretend to be a writer, exclusively, of one sort or the other. Automatic writing is an attempted purity of wildness as was (mendaciously, it turns out) Allen Ginsberg's first-thought-best-thought aesthetic. The wild men and women (understandably often American) believe the critic is Censor by any other name. Read Emerson, experience Whitman, discover Blake, convince yourself that your barbaric yawp, your primal scream, will be your highest-holiest sound. Alternatively, become critic entire – as did Europhile Yvor Winters, Allen Tate, William Empson, and, one might argue, wild-fearing, Emerson-Whitman-Blake-denying T. S. Eliot.

I am aware that, throughout this essay, I have assumed a fairly untheorized notion of literary greatness; and that's something I do believe in – although it is easier to define than defend. *Great writing, like all great art, is that which has the capacity to*

fascinate the future. Not the abstract future, but the individual people of the years to come who pay passionate attention to writing. It is possible that there will be only a very few of these people, and that there is almost no reason writing for them. There is no way to second-guess what will fascinate the future, but it seems to me that one of the enduring reasons for reading is to have intimate contact with people from a different historical period; we read the Victorians because we want to read their epoch through them, and them through their epoch. Therefore, writing that most engages with its own moment, without the caveat of worrying whether it will be comprehensible in ten years' time, without anticipating and trying to forestall footnotes, will be the most likely to fascinate. Aiming for the literary is not a reliable method of writing what turns out in the end to be literature. The only way that the writing of the past (summarized as "literary values") can be learnt from is as an encouragement to pursue the oddest hares. Literary history is an object lesson in favourites fallen and weird and unlikely survivals: take Solzhenitsyn, once widely seen as the most important contemporary writer, now a living curio; take Blake, once a failure, now an Immortal. The cautious, the sensible – these engage us far less than the outrageously unexpected. Yet if our own epoch comes to be seen as one of the dull patches which exist in the past, then our writing, whatever its ambitions to be great, will go unread. Just as the smooth numbers of the age of Dryden seem aesthetically irrelevant now, so the strident innovation-mongering of the twentieth century will perhaps come one day soon to seem uninteresting. A thought-experiment I sometimes try is to imagine that we live not in a belated age, as writers since before Homer have felt, but that we are actually primitives. Granted another two thousand years (a lot to grant, I admit), we will seem as far distant as the gospels. With the likelihood of some major genetic intervention, what makes humanity is about to change. To the future, we are likely to seem charmingly random: with our chaotic comings-to-birth, our haphazard childhoods, our emotional traumas, we will appear almost feral. To report truly on this awkward present, though probably no more awkward than all those past presents, is one of the hardest things a writer can attempt. We can explain ourselves away in a second (I have an addictive personality; I'm lower middle class; I've got bad genes) or we can participate in the oddness of enacted selfhood. The question may be better reversed, as almost-nonsense:

Where does my inspiration get me from?

✒

Doubleblind

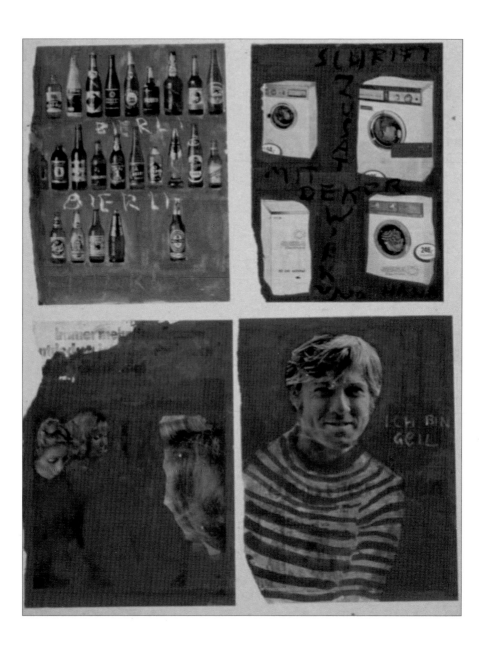

For the deaf war they're waging:
Contemporary Romanian and Bessarabian Poetry

FIONA SAMPSON

> Writers die. Poets die. Of course.
> Of course. Now they're just cannon fodder
> for the deaf war they're waging.

(Marta Petreu, "The Country's Rush Toward Red", tr. Brenda Walker)

After the revolution which led to the fall of Ceausescu in 1989, the newly-open Romania acquired a kind of notoriety. A country, all of whose twenty-six million inmates had been brutalised and half-starved, became known, particularly in the West, for its treatment of unwanted and orphaned children. Improvement – left to market forces and many of the same corrupt officials who had always been in power – has been slow since then; perhaps because of this, 1989 marked no particular watershed in poetic style, although it did change the conditions under which writers could publish. It's only very recently, since the ten-year anniversary of the revolution marked just how little progress of any kind had been made, that a new generation of turbulent young voices has emerged, especially in Bessarabia.

Romanian is a Romance language, reasonably easy to read with the help of a dictionary for anyone who has ever learnt French, Italian, Latin. However, its Latin orthography wasn't regulated till 1881, during the period in which Romanian national identity, like that of many other European states, was established. This was also the era of the national poet Mihai Eminescu (1850–1889). The only non-Slav Balkan culture, Romania is still regarded as part of the *Francophonie* – although French is the second language of educated urbanites only, there's quite a traffic of translation both in Romania and in France – and those quarters of old Bucharest not flattened by Ceausescu are characterised by elegant *belle époque* architecture. Minority communities – of which the most sizeable is that of the one-and-a-half million Hungarians in the contested territory of Transylvania – also include, despite Ceausescu's attempts at ethnic cleansing, German-speaking Saxons, Ukrainians, Armenians (such as the novelist Agopian), and a small number of Jews (including, among poets, Emil Brumaru, Gheorghe Schwarz, and the great surrealist Gellu Naum, who died last year). Members of these communities

BEFORE THE FLOWERS
OF FRIENDSHIP FADED
FRIENDSHIP FADED

often publish in their mother tongues. The centre for Hungarian publishing, for example, is the Transylvanian university town of Brasov, where the lyric miniaturist Attila Sántha is based. There are also nearly half a million Roma; recently Luminita Mihai Cioaba, the daughter of a *bulibasha* (chief), emerged as a writer who is working out of their oral traditions.

Romanian-language poetry itself is a strange mixture of cultural homogeneity and exuberant invention. It displays the easy, rapid movement and lack of inflecting register of other Romance poetries; though unlike con-temporary French and Italian poetics, in particular, it isn't characterised by abstract thought so much as the record of experience. Strikingly for the con-temporary British ear, most present-day Romanian poetry doesn't describe a particular concrete reality but uses metaphor – extended into symbolism and even to the point of surrealism – to evoke experiences which are often existential. Consider Ioan Es. Pop's "Baptism":

> there's a clock in the room and hans is feeding it secretly.
> move faster, he whispers to it, c'mon, move faster.
> he bought it a shirt and dressed it. he
> washes it changes it takes care of it like the eyes in his head.
> but the clock is sleepy. it's put on weight, grown as large as
> the table. it can hardly stand on its own legs.
>
> (Tr. Nathaniel Smith, *et al.*)

An evocation which resists explanation, such poetry works best as a willed disordering of expectation. If the childishness of this bad-fairytale imagery is subversive, so is the punctuation. It's not only the lack of capital letters which keeps this stanza moving rapidly as if towards incoherence: it's also that unpunctuated list which seems to burst into exaggeration. Both strategies – the use of fairytale and grammatical subversion – recur in contemporary Romanian poetry, especially in the work of other members of the particularly strong generation, born in the late '50s, to which Pop belongs.

This generation's undoubted leader is now the art historian Magda Carneci, who works in Paris and whose latest work is strongly influenced by French philosophy. Her characteristic flying long lines could be tricksy if each fragmenting phrase wasn't such a clear indictment of the – gendered? globalised? – experience of objectification:

> We stayed   fixed on beds   immaculate wet white surfaces
>   we stay in the photos and wait   for somebody to come
>   to raise us up   to plunge us in the zinc basin   of strong cold acids

     to develop us   to fix us in poses   or expose us to an even stronger light
a purer light   to fog us   to blind us
and destroy us at last   these dark old negatives
     beauty   the great happening   to save the earth   or make it vanish.
(Translated by the poet with Adam Sorkin)

On the other hand, her peer Mircea Cartarescu draws fragments of a disintegrating experience together into a lyric, often highly-sexualised whole:

> you're like a peacock with bucharest fanned out behind you
> hotels blinking, women sparkling, the very cobblestones
> graduating in cybernetics […]
> ("It Was a Time of Flowers", tr. Simion Dumitrache *et al.*)

In sharp contrast is Mariana Marin, who died earlier this summer at the age of forty-seven. Marin had an extraordinary reputation among her contemporaries as a political witness in both life and work: her health permanently damaged as a result. Her poetry is as vividly declamatory as that of these contemporaries; but it is also shorter, tightly-focussed, and overtly political: "And so, poverty and death, / how they drag us after them / in immense nets of nerves…" ("Elegy VII" tr. Adam J. Sorkin and Mia Nazarie.)

Earlier books included *The Secret Wing*, a poetic dialogue with Anne Frank which allowed Marin to find an extended metaphor for Romanian life under dictatorship. In the late '80s she could be published only in France. Her *Elegies* date from this time:

> I invite you to run away with me into the abyss that has been given us.
> Once there, your freckles and your red hair
> will surely take the hint and love
> the language of my breasts
>
> between which, even then, death will lie all night long.
> ("Elegy XII" tr. Adam J. Sorkin and Angela Jianu)

Marin – like another of her contemporaries, Marta Petreu – has a compact clarity of diction, almost like direct speech, which makes both of them inheritors of a tradition. Along with the poet and editor Denisa Comanescu, and the slightly-older Grete Tartler (whose *Orient Express* we have in Fleur Adcock's translation) they adopt a faintly mandarin understatement: one in which ellipsis prefigures the radical slippages of Carneci and quietitude prefigures Cartarescu's comprehensive lyric. It's a tradition Marin Sorescu

(1936–1996) secured as an editor-critic and, eventually, as Minister of Culture. His contemporary Nichita Stanescu (1933-1983), equally influential as an editor and Romania's foremost poet from the '60s onwards, both secured and challenged these conventions; his intensely confessional verse a modernising force in its risk-taking diction rather than in its overt political message. Though Sorescu's public role may have secured him translation in the west, it is the hugely prolific Stanescu whose influence is acknowledged throughout contemporary Balkan writing. His influence on younger Romanian poets born in the '60s and '70s is particularly marked.

But who are the bridges to this generation? A group of surprising women individualists, all of whom we're lucky to have had in single-author collections in Britain: Nina Cassian (b. 1927), Ana Blandiana (b. 1942), Ioana Ieronim (b. 1947) and Liliana Ursu (b. 1949). Cassian, who has lived in the States for nearly twenty years, has had perhaps the widest influence on British poets, maybe because of the purity of her diction: "Something glitters, I don't know / whether it's a needle / or a splinter from my bone" ("Echo", tr. Andrea Deletant and Brenda Walker). By contrast with these miniatures, Blandiana presents a world in which everything is constantly mobile, even the act of "Falling Asleep":

> The sky is soft and leaves on the fingers
> A sort of pollen.
> Over our faces move
> The shadows of flocks of birds,
> The smell of grapes seeps into us.
> (tr. Andrea Deletant and Brenda Walker)

Ieronim's verse-memoir of the ethnic cleansing of rural Saxon communities from Transylvania in the mid-twentieth century, *The Triumph of the Water Witch*, is narrated with the simultaneous clarity and mystification of a child's-eye-view:

> People and things reappeared on the dial of the days, after hours of air water fire earth. Tower clocks of leaves and wind. After the muffled res-onance of the organ and flutes. Evening shadows across bridges.

Water Witch is translated by Adam Sorkin, who has become the chief translator, and thereby advocate, of Romanian poetry into English, especially since the retirement of Brenda Walker of the sadly-missed Forest Books. This is not a trivial point, since only adventurous, sensitive translations can recreate whole poetries for non-native readers. We can't rely on the happy accident of particular poets' enthusiasms. This said, for the Romanians, Fleur Adcock, Alan Brownjohn and Tess Gallagher have all acted as poetic ambassadors to the Anglophone world. It was Gallagher and Sorkin, for example, who together translated a selection of Liliana Ursu's strikingly concrete, proverbial – in fact oddly Central European – poems as *The Sky Behind the Forest*. Several of these poetic enthusiasms were fostered by the British Council's policy of bringing British writers to Romania, and it's to be hoped this policy won't disappear before younger generations, on both sides of the European divide, have had a chance to find each other's work.

Two of the brightest young Romanian women poets are currently in forms of economic exile in North America. Diana Manole (b.1963), who emigrated to Canada in 2000, creates, in "The Surgeon's Nightmare", an anti-nursery of folk tale and symbol gone violently adrift:

> The soft white fur snake slides discreetly between the spines of the books.
> Birds knot their striped woollen mufflers to spare their vocal chords
> and granddads sculpt their crutches and splints
> decorating them with the symbols of sun and moon.

Like Saviana Stanescu (b. 1967), who is studying in the US, Manole is also a playwright; both are fascinated by the play of illusory and multiple personae, as here in Stanescu's "Infanta Margherita":

> shut tight in a music box its walls lined
> with finest silk they nailed her foot
> to the gold velvet floor
> round and round she turns crying *mar-ghe-ri-ta*
> people laugh how cute how cute
> (tr. Adam J. Sorkin)

This is postmodernism with an edge which contemporary Bessarabian poets sharpen yet further. Vsevolod Ciornei seizes on it for his "Arson Poetica" – "Hunger reads the newspaper / I'm paraphrasing so a horse could get it / Hunger is illiterate / (here I'm introducing my element of paradox)" – and Nicolae Leahu for a difficult love:

> parts of speech – our bodies
>
> I seek you through meanings in the Romanian tongue
> you're a difficult word to utter with the body
> an improper name
> ("Poems for My: 6", tr. Adam J. Sorkin and Cristina Cirstea)

But it's triumphantly exploded by the extraordinary and inventive Emilian Galaicu-Paun:

> [...] an expansive poetry an endless poetry just like
> latitude 66° 33′ North the poem goes round and round.
> we have been deported beyond the artic circle of thought we subjects
> > with warm
> blood in our hearts where transcendence descends from the sky
> ("Vacca", tr. Adam J. Sorkin and Cristina Cirstea)

Galaicu-Paun's long lines, subversive punctuation, and grasp of myth bring "round" again several of the poetic strategies with which this brief survey started. They indicate the extent to which Romanian and Bessarabian poetries are capable of both adaptive regeneration and strongly-sustained cultural identity. They are poetries of huge cultural confidence and energetic invention, which show no sign of diminishing.

*

Further reading:
Andrei Bodiu, Romulus Bucur, Georgeta Moarcas (editors), *Romanian Poets of the 80s and 90s* (Editura Paralela 45, Pitesti, 1999).
Eveline L. Kanes and Mihai Zaharia (translators), *My Country, My Language: Ten Romanian Poets* (Romanian Cultural Foundation, Bucharest, 1999).
Fiona Sampson (editor), *Orient Express: the best of contemporary writing from Enlargement Europe* Vol I /II (Carneci, Ieronim, Manole: Oxford, 2002), Vol III (Galaicu-Paun, Crasnaru: 2003).
Ioan Stoica (editor), Brenda Walker (translator), *Young Poets of a New Romania* (Forest Books, London, 1991).
Adam J. Sorkin, Cristina Cirstea and Sean Cotter (editors), *Singular Destinies: Contemporary Poets of Bessarabia* (Cartier, Chisinau, 2003).
Adam J. Sorkin and Kurt W. Treptow (editors), *An Anthology of Romanian Women Poets East European Monographs* (Columbia University Press, New York, 1994).

After a gap of six years the Poetry Society is delighted to relaunch the European poetry translation prize, with a new sponsor and a new title. **The Corneliu M Popescu Prize for European Poetry Translation**, sponsored by the Ratiu Family Charitable Foundation, was launched in March this year. The judges were Alan Brownjohn and Fleur Adcock. There was a greater than expected number of entries, but finally a decision was reached, and David Constantine's translation of Hans Magnus Enzensberger's *Lighter Than Air* (Bloodaxe) was the winner.

"Reality stricken / With homesickness":

The poetry of Laura Riding

PATRICK MCGUINNESS

To say that Laura Riding's poetry set itself an impossible task and failed would be a mistake of emphasis; rather, she set poetry an impossible task and it failed her. "Renouncing" it in the early 1940s, she gave up (and gave up on) poetry as a means of attaining what she called – without inverted commas, dramatic pauses or ironic self-distancing – truth. The preface to her *Collected Poems* (1938) is an ambitious defence of the function of poetry. However, by the time this collection (her chosen "canon") re-appears in 1980 as *The Poems of Laura Riding*, it comes equipped also with a preface explaining why she stopped writing poetry, and several postfaces and appendices reiterating her reasons. As her preface to *Selected Poems: In Five Sets* (1970) indicates, Riding saw her poems as at once poetry's highest expression and its most complete summation of failure:

> I judge my poems to be things of the first water as poetry, but that does not make them better than poetry, and I think poetry obstructs general attainment to something better in our linguistic way-of-life than we have. I can only hope that the poems themselves will soften this incon-sistency by making the nature of poetry, to which they are faithful, plainer, in its forced, fine suspension of truth; poetry and truth have both been so much hashed that there is little whole perception of what they are.

In her great late-period work, *Rational Meaning: A New Foundation for the Definition of Words,* Riding wrote that her "objective in poetry may be said to have gone beyond the poetic as a literary category and reached over into the field of the general human ideal in speaking . . .". These are great and distracting claims: the books and essays in which she outlined her reasons for giving up writing poetry have come to form a kind of secondary literature of renunciation, often read over (and occasionally instead of) the poems themselves.

Laura Riding was born Laura Reichenthal in New York in 1901. She studied at Cornell, where she began publishing poetry, notably in the *Fugitive* magazine, founded and edited by a group that included John Crowe Ransom and Allen Tate. It was these poets who in 1924 awarded Laura Riding

Gottschalk (she had by then married and this was her first author name) the Nashville poetry prize. Her first collection, *The Close Chaplet*, appeared in 1926 (the British edition was published by Leonard and Virginia Woolf at the Hogarth Press). During this period, Robert Graves encountered her work and included her poem "The Quids" in his book *Contemporary Techniques of Poetry: A Political Analogy* (1925). The two had corresponded but first met in January 1926, beginning a literary collaboration lasting some fourteen years, during half of which they lived in Deya, Majorca, where they ran their Seizin Press (which published, among much else, Gertrude Stein's *An Acquaintance with Description*, 1929, and the journal *Epilogue*,1935–8). Their best-known literary collaboration, *A Survey of Modernist Poetry*, appeared in 1927. In 1939, back in America, Riding met Schuyler Jackson, a poet and poetry editor at *Time* magazine who had favourably reviewed her work (among his compliments was that every word in her poems attained its "fullest literal meaning"). In 1941 they married, settling eventually in Wabasso, Florida. Together they began work on a *Dictionary of Exact Meanings*, whose ambition was to provide single unambiguous definitions for twenty-four thousand words ("one meaning, one word", was the mission), without recourse to synonymity (synonyms led to imprecision by connecting words by similarity rather than distinctness) or etymology (which maintained the authority of usage however erroneous). They set themselves a target of 100 words a week, but since many words needed definition up to 200 times, the project became self-defeating. Riding and Jackson have often been presented as a two-person Sisyphus of semantics, but this would be wrong, since from the ruin of the enterprise there emerged *Rational Meaning: A New Foundation for the Definition of Words*, a work of extraordinary (and unparaphraseable) ambition. The book remained unpublished during their lifetimes (Schuyler died in 1968, she in 1991), but finally appeared in 1997. Several of its concerns were aired in 1972 in *The Telling*, a book whose admirers included such different poet-critics as Donald Davie and Charles Bernstein, who has called *Rational Meaning* an "anti-poetics". Riding called *The Telling* her "personal evangel", and it has the quality not of a lecture or a sermon, but of an imparting.

Laura Riding was already, before encountering Graves, an acute critic; in later years, her work (especially the *Survey of Modernist Poetry*) was considered germane to the development of the New Criticism. Riding did not entirely discount the claim, but distanced her work from what she called "the gospel of ambiguity" popularised by William Empson. In *A Survey*, she and Graves had written "The poem is not the paper, not the type, not the spoken syllables. It is as invisible and inaudible as thought…". More ambitiously, Riding wrote in *Anarchism is Not Enough* (1928):

> What is a poem? A poem is nothing. By persistence the poem can be made something; but then it is something, not a poem. Why is it nothing? Because it cannot be looked at, heard, touched or read (what can be read is prose). It is not an effect (common or uncommon) of experience; it is the result of an ability to create a vacuum in experience – it is a vacuum and therefore nothing. It cannot be looked at, heard, touched or read...

Anarchism is Not Enough is not just a book of literary criticism, but a book of theory in which we see emerging themes which were to define Riding's poetry and thought in the decades to come:

> A poem is made out of nothing by a nobody – made out of a socially non-existent element in language. [...] Poetry appeals only to poetry and begets nothing but poetry. [...] The end of poetry is not an after-effect, not a pleasurable memory of itself, but an immediate, constant and even unpleasant insistence on itself; indeed, it has no end. [...] Poetry brings all possible experience to the same degree: a degree in the consciousness beyond which the consciousness itself cannot go. Poetry is defeat, the end which is not an end but a stopping-short because it is impossible to go further; it makes mad; it is the absolutism of dissatisfaction. [...] Poetry therefore seems idle, sterile, narrow, destroying. And it is. This is what recommends it.

Poetry, for Riding, is the hard path, the art that takes one to the limit, that finds the world broken and reorders it into final form – final in the sense that once done there is nothing left but contemplation.

Riding's early ("non-canonical") poems (those collected in *First Awakenings* and written between 1920 and 1926) feel already stripped down, ascetic, austere. "A City Seems" is one of these:

> A city seems between us. It is only love,
> Love like a sorrow still
> After a labor, after light.
> The crowds are one.
> Sleep is a single heart
> Filling the old avenues we used to know
> With miracles of dark and dread
> We dare not go to meet
> Save as our own dead stalking

Or as two dreams walking
One tread and terrible,
One cloak of longing in the cold,
Though we stand separate and wakeful
Measuring death in miles between us
Where a city seems and memories
Sleep like a populace.

The poem's rigour, its certainty of tone, its precision even as it articulates inner complexities, are unusual for a poet in her apprenticeship. It is also difficult to see what might have influenced its execution. It is spare, ascetic, and displays a certain faith that words like "love" and "a sorrow" mean exactly what they say. The language is limpid and clear; its difficulty comes not from unusual locutions or specialised words, but from forceful but unexpected syntactical turns, and from the stretching of sense units across short irregular lines. Big words go unelaborated – "Love" is undefined, as if it were enough to experience the emotion to the full for it to become universally communicable; as she wrote in "Echoes": "Love is very everything, like fire:/ Many things burning, / But only one combustion". Such poetry seems to be written with the apparently untroubled certainty that it will be understood. There is a similarity here to Mallarmé's "tone", which, like Riding's, often seems an amalgam of the hieratic and the matter-of-fact.

Another poem from *First Awakenings*, "Evasions", displays these characteristics more clearly. The opening is arresting, playing off the colloquial assertiveness of the tone against the audacity of the proposition:

Streets move evasively and so do people.
Both chew their covert cuds and yet they are
Quite different. For streets have consciences
At street-corners and spit their cuds there at
The curb with lamp-posts for confessors.

But people only swallow theirs and go
To hide in houses, fearing edges and
Sharp turnings that might bring them face to face
With unexpected honesties or yet
A sudden crying ordinance to halt
Their apprehensive slinking in the streets
And call them fiercely to encounters there
With one another's eyes and ponderings.

And yet, because they go so nervously
And do not stop for scrutiny, shall we
Call caution furtiveness or rather say
That shunning candor, they find sanity.

"Evasions" is hard to contextualise – where does a poem like this "come from"? What are its influences? It is unmistakeably in Riding's voice, and bears the stamp of her thought, but shares something with the "alienating modernist city" poem, for which all sorts of models existed. "Evasions" announces at once its relationship of subject with, and its distinctiveness of execution from, a prevailing mode. Riding could have taken a sub-Eliotic approach and packed her poem with scrambled mutterings or the boom of some evasive oracle; or she could have followed the voice-throwing ironies of a range of Baudelaire-impregnated city poems, packing it with symbols, images or naturalistic detail. Instead, her poem seems to arrive owing nothing to anybody: it is sharp and hard-edged: the voice that directs it and the con-sciousness that guides it are unsplintered, even as they describe the splintering of experience.

Riding's early poems are inward but not introspective, intimate but not private. The further inwards they go, the more authoritative and impersonal their tone, piecing the world together not through metaphors or similes, but through acts of intellectual synthesis. These acts constitute the poems, poems that seem to have reached beyond figurative language without having passed through it first. Pound talked of logopoeia as the "dance of the intellect among words"; Riding's poems seem more of a purposeful march.

II

The question of whether Riding's poetry has the abandonment of poetry written into it in advance, like fate into a Greek tragedy, has been central to the way she is read. However, it's important to realise that these poems say and do things that could only be said and done (or "enacted") in poetry – things that would not exist or be known were it not for their *poetic* expression. Many of Riding's poems enact forms of revelation, or account for revelations missed and understandings thwarted, as in "Hospitality to Words":

The small the far away
The unmeant meanings
Of sincere conversation
Encourage the common brain of talkers
And steady the cup-handles on the table.

Over the rims the drinking eyes
Taste close congratulation
And are satisfied.

Happy room, meal of securities,
The fire distributes feelings,
The cross-beam showers down centuries.
How mad for friendliness
Creep words from where they shiver and starve,
Small and far away in thought,
Untalkative and outcast.

Words are exiled from their meanings even as they are uttered, split off from their true selves as from the true selves of their utterers. As in many of Riding's poems, there is an unusual visual, even dramatic, presentation of abstract phenomena. These are philosophical arguments acted out in verse, yet these poems are not allegorical; there are no symbols; nothing "stands in" for something else. In *Rational Meaning*, she recalls explaining herself to another writer; what she describes is, in its dramatic conception, its compression and its air of moral imperative, almost the plot for "Hospitality to Words":

> I wrote . . . on how people make words enemies by using them against their character as instruments of truth – as which they are *friends*. I described [words] as escaping their users, when not so used[,] as "leaving only husks in the hands of the fools and liars – remaining themselves intact, not really used".

Sometimes Riding achieves a tone of such commanding sureness that we have a sense of experiencing something at once mysterious and completely self-explanatory, as in "Death as Death":

> To conceive death as death
> Is difficulty come by easily,
> A blankness fallen among
> Images of understanding,
> Death like a quick cold hand
> On the hot slow head of suicide.
> So is it come by easily
> For one instant. Then again furnaces
> Roar in the ears, then again hell revolves,
> And the elastic eye holds paradise

At visible length from blindness,
And dazedly the body echoes
"Like this, like this, like nothing else."

Like nothing – a similarity
Without resemblance. The prophetic eye,
Closing upon difficulty,
Opens upon comparison,
Halving the actuality
As a gift too plain, for which
Gratitude has no language,
Foresight no vision.

The poem pits actuality and literal understanding against mediated knowledge and false comprehension: the ways in which we make sense of death, piecing it together by means of what we know rather than coming to it in its fearful uniqueness. "Comparison" is, here, what falsely smoothes away the "difficulty". The actuality of death is "halved" by comparison (rather as a word defined by synonymity loses what makes it unique by emphasising what makes it like another), offering only a moment's solace, before, in that marvellously-caught rush of danger and confusion, "furnaces / Roar in the ears", "hell again revolves". Riding works by antithesis and paradox – "difficulty come by easily", "visible length from blindness", "similarity without resemblance". Her poems are full of distinctions between forms of genuine apprehension, articulation and enactment, and their impostors: distinctions between speaking and talking, self and image, understandings and false understandings.

One of her most famous poems, "The Unthronged Oracle" uses images of reflections and projections to convey the mind's progress and return upon itself:

[...]
Your coming, asking, seeing, knowing,
Was a fleeing from and stumbling
Into only mirrors, and behind which
Behind all mirrors, dazzling pretences,
The general light of fortune
Keeps wrapt in sleeping unsleeep,
All-mute of time, self-muttering like mute:
Fatality like lone wise-woman
Her unbought secrets counting over
That stink of hell, from fuming in her lap. [...]

Though Riding rarely neologises, she coins compounds of her own – "unsleep", "all-mute", "self-muttering" – and in poems like "Come Words Away" shows herself conscious of the oracular tone her poetry often takes:

> [...]
> Come, words, away to where
> The meaning is not thickened
> With the voice's fretting substance,
> Nor look of words is curious
> As letters in books staring out
> All that man ever thought strange
> And laid to sleep on white
> Like the archaic manuscript
> Of dreams at morning blacked on wonder. [...]

Here voice "thicken[s]" meaning, with its implications of coarsening and blunting, the false lure of "self"-expression. This most obviously corrresponds to Riding's notion of personal voice interposing itself between utterance and expression. Where the early Riding believed that poetry could overcome this barrier, the later Riding (of her "second understanding") came to see poetry as the problem, not the solution, "[telling] differently for the triumph of difference, and not for truth's sake" ("The Telling"). Riding is an "impersonal" poet, provided we see this over-used adjective not as denoting merely the abolition of personal voice, but the enlargement of voice until it expresses more than itself. In "Second-Death" Riding writes about the unequal relationship between original and copy, between life and its image:

> Far roam the death-faces
> From the face-shaped lockets,
> The small oval tombs of truth,
> In second-death, the portrait sadness.
>
> Long hunger the death-faces to know
> Who was once who and hear hello
> And be remembered as so-and-so
> Where albums keep
> Death like a sleep.
>
> First-death, life unlikeness,
> Second-death, life-likeness
> And portrait sadness,

Continuous hope and haunting,
Reality stricken
With homesickness.

"Reality stricken / With homesickness" is a beautiful line, and could stand alone as an expression of Riding's desire to reintegrate the sundered whole through language. Her attitude, here and elsewhere, towards art (the poem, the portrait, the image) is that it often captures what is least true or least relevant; the death-likeness of the merely lifelike – hence the frequency in her work of idols, graven images, false representations and empty reflections.

III

In the journal *Chelsea* in 1962, Riding referred to the "whorl of poetic artifice, with its overpowering necessities of patterned rhythm and harmonic sound-play, which work distortions upon the natural proprieties of tone and word". Like much modernist poetry (from which it differs), Riding's work suggests (or brings one to) a kind of linguistic limit-situation. But it does so on its own terms. For Riding, language is perfectly sufficient; it is poetry that is not. She is unwilling to exploit poetry's insufficiency for her (and its) own ends. For many poets, poetry is at its truest and most expressive when confronting its own limits, or articulating how the real, the experienced or the imagined exceeds or eludes language. Much of the greatest modern poetry, from Baudelaire and Mallarmé to Eliot and Wallace Stevens, has been poetry that gestures to its own beyond, works with its short-comings, its "non-meeting" with what obsesses it. In this way poetry capitalises expressively on language's presumed expressive shortfall – from Baudelaire decribing himself as a "painter condemned to paint on clouds" to Eliot's "raid on the inarticulate / With shabby equipment always deteriorat-ing". Laura Riding refuses these and related attitudes as so much rhetoric and bad faith. She wrote scathingly of Eliot's "boast of wringing from [language] signal successes of expression despite its shameful inadequacies", and claimed that modernist poetry's "imputation to language of an intrinsic defectiveness [was] part of the rhetoric of late human criticism of the human inheritance". It is not language and truth, but poetry and truth that are the parallel worlds that fail to meet, as Riding once wrote, "by a moment, and a word".

Like all who seem to demand complete assent, Laura Riding is easy to disagree with. But there is no bad faith in her work: her writing wants to be understood, even if the things it speaks of are difficult to understand or beyond understanding. She is a "difficult" poet, but not one who sought out difficulty, or attached any prestige to it. She wrote of faithfulness and constancy being prerequisites for enlightened reading, and the terms in which she expresses her thought are a mix of religion and pragmatics, combining a spiritual sense of the revelatory or truth-telling potential of language with a technical, almost scientific approach to the foundedness and communicability of meaning. As she puts it in *Rational Meaning*, we have "unlearned" or "fallen away" from language (those religious overtones are integral to her sense). Like a body that passes through a wall or irrevocably changes substance, her poetry takes itself to a point of no return, or a point at which it cannot return as poetry. It has become commonplace to talk about writing "beyond" poetry; in Riding's case it may be applicable, but only if we recognise that she had to write through poetry first, and that for us as readers of poetry that "through" is of more interest than any beyond.

A Survey of Modernist Poetry and A Pamphlet Against Anthologies by Laura Riding and Robert Graves. Reprinted by permission of Carcanet Press, Manchester, 1927, 1928; 2002, and the author's Board of Literary Management. *Anarchism is not Enough* by Laura Riding. Reprinted by permission of University of California Press, 1928; 2001 and the author's Board of Literary Management. "A City Seems" and "Evasions" from *First Awakenings: The Early Poems*, by Laura Riding. Reprinted by permission of Carcanet Press, Manchester, 1992, and the author's Board of Literary Management. *Rational Meaning: A New Foundation for the Definition of Words* by Laura (Riding) Jackson. Reprinted by permission of University Press of Virginia, 1997, and the author's Board of Literary management. "Hospitality to Words", "Death as Death", "The Unthronged Oracle", "Come Words Away", "Second Death" from *The Poems of Laura Riding: A New Edition of the 1938 Collection*, by Laura (Riding) Jackson, Persea Books, New York. Reprinted by permission of Carcanet Press, Manchester, 1980; 2001 and the author's Board of Literary Management.

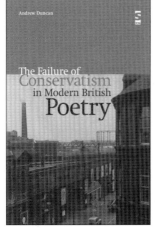

Reviews

Keeping fit and keeping moving

Liz Lochhead, *The Colour of Black & White: Poems 1984–2003*,
Polygon, ISBN 0954407520
Dreaming Frankenstein & Collected Poems 1967–1984,
Polygon, £8.99, ISBN 0748661581

With *Dreaming Frankenstein* and *The Colour of Black & White* Liz Lochhead collects over three decades of work. In the author's own modest phrase, these are poems written "for consolation, and for fun"; but the thirty-year journey has been a long and interesting one, and the poems are more substantial than Lochhead's self-deprecation might suggest.

Although English and drama were important to Lochhead at the Motherwell secondary school she attended – where she wrote the best essays and won the lead parts in school plays – against her headmaster's advice she left not for university but for the Glasgow School of Art. That was in 1965, when abstraction was exercising the minds of students and teachers alike at Glasgow. Open to the appreciation of abstract forms, Lochhead nevertheless felt that her own figurative sensibility and working practice could not find a grounding in the contemporary milieu. So it was, in turn, art that pushed her back to language. Attending several encouraging workshops by the poet and playwright Stephen Mulrine, based in the Liberal Arts Department, and then, after graduating with a Diploma in Drawing and Painting, occasionally participating in the different workshops run by Philip Hobsbaum and Tom McGrath, Lochhead found that poetry had become extremely important to her, and that she was very good at writing it. With the success of her first book *Memo to Spring* (1972), which sold 1,500 copies in a few months – this in a market a tenth the size of England's – she also found herself actively at the heart of a Glasgow literary renaissance.

It is difficult to overestimate the importance of the first half of the 1970s to contemporary Scottish literature, and of Glasgow at this time in particular. It is also hard to prise apart the different forms – poetry, the novel, the short story, performance art and drama – that would all intermingle in any account of the period. There is a pre-history to it, with Edwin Morgan's heterogeneous *The Second Life* (1968) a presiding spirit, and Alexander Trocchi and Kenneth White being hard man and shaman bookends at the wobbly edges of the Glasgow canon. Before Morgan's extraordinary example, and the unsettling novels of George Friel, there was also the post-war reconstruction exemplified by the poetry and arts publisher William McLellan. Yet out of those writers' workshops thirty years ago came authors whose work has driven the much more recent and sometimes more popular successes in Scottish fiction and poetry. Alan Warner, Jackie Kay, Janice Galloway, Irvine Welsh, Donny O'Rourke, Ali Smith, Robert Crawford, Kathleen Jamie, David Kinloch, Peter McCarey, and Peter Manson have surely emerged and become their individual writing selves in significant part through the work of Alasdair Gray, James Kelman, Tom Leonard, Alan Spence, and Liz Lochhead, even if one or two others less known from this critical period, such as James McGonigal, are still to receive their due. It has not all been a Glasgow thing, of course, especially as far as the leading poetry magazines are concerned, most of which were, and are, Edinburgh based. It is also notable that Lochhead has cited the crafted Edinburgh voice of Robert Garioch, a master of the sonnet, as one of her principal influences. America and European translation have had their part to play, too. But it is fascinating that for a city, unlike the capital, which to this day has a relatively poor publishing infrastructure, Glasgow should have such a good writing one.

Such a context for Lochhead's poetry might seem to lead towards debates about realism and "authentic voice" in her work. Kelman and Leonard in particular are sometimes championed as working class realists, as if the myth of tough Glasgow, real Glasgow, has to be overlaid on each and every Glasgow writer's work. But Kelman's work employs a high degree of stylisation, making comparisons with the director David Mamet's speech patterning as appropriate as any appeal to grit. Similarly, Leonard's early and continuing interest in sound poetry, and the sophisticated visual/oral disjunctions in his own verse, make it a grave mistake to see his work within the normal bounds of realism, as if his poetry were the transcripts of a miked-up undercover snoop.

This is not to diminish these writers' sensitivity to the spoken word and there is certainly an interest in the speaking voice in Lochhead's poems. Another volume that would further mark the scale of Lochhead's achievement would be a selection of her many works for theatre, outstandingly the ensemble piece *Mary Queen of Scots Got Her Head Chopped Off* (1987) and *Quelques Fleurs* (1991), whose central character, the voracious consumer Verena, was originally played by Lochhead herself. Clearly the spoken word occupies the borderlands between her poetry and her drama, and that is a territory she shares with her friend Carol Ann Duffy, dedicatee of several poems in *The Colour of Black & White*. Lochhead's 1981 collection *The Grimm Sisters,* an exploration of fairy tale and archetypal women, often in their own imagined voices, may well have created aesthetic space which Duffy has been able to develop. Others have learnt from the slightly more oblique elements of Lochhead's poetry, especially its examination and lyric reinvigoration of common sayings, "true clichés", and here the Jo Shapcott of *Phrasebook* certainly suggests productive kinship.

In interview Lochhead has been rightly reluctant to have her poems categorised as "for performance". Her drama is certainly poetic, but not in the slightly limp, worthy way that "poetic" can sometimes mean when allied to the stage. Rather, it manages to utilise a great range of registers as well as interpolations from other forms, from playground rhymes to proprietary names, and is not always shy of attaining a higher, more sonorous language. Some of her poems certainly do read as if in character, which is one kind of performance, although usually, as with the short staccato sentences of "Spinster" (1981), which affectionately parody self-help advice, the effect is not linear but something rather fuller, rather more complex, as with the image of elastication holding body and soul together: "My life's in shards. / I'll keep fit in leotards". Other poems have a propelling rhythm, where character is not so important as fleetfoot wit, another kind of performance. Even if the provisional and rather condescending category of "performance" is accepted, and also acknowledging the curse and gift of Scottish poetry's social context, in which poems are under a burden of both conviviality and benign teacherliness, then these are fine poems; but viewed in that way they are not the half of what Lochhead offers.

From early on there has been both an interest in and a resistance to the lyric, so that in the near title poem, "Memo to Myself for Spring", the persona describes the threatening "forest of cosmetic counters" as "lyric poetry". In another poem of that period, "Object" (1972), despite an occasional prosiness, parallels can be found with the practice and politics of some in the more direct-speaking elements of those associated, rightly or wrongly, with the Cambridge school: "I am limited. In whose likeness / do you reassemble me? / [...] It's a fixed attitude you / force me into. / Cramp knots calf muscles; / pins and needles rankle in my arm; / my shoulder aches; / irked, I am aware of my extremities". This looks forward both to later Denise Riley (although Lochhead seems to have subsequently left cooler enquiry for others), and to Duffy's "Standing Female Nude".

By the time of *Dreaming Frankenstein* (1984), Lochhead's hesitancy towards, and self-conscious examination of, the lyric self has become both more relaxed and more confident: "Hafiz on Danforth Avenue" nods to Frank O'Hara, Hafiz, and Edwin Morgan without being overcome by them, without losing its reality as a love poem, and "A Gift" risks some very abstract nouns "I see / when well-meaning / other lovers brought you their gifthorses of nightmare & / selfhatred you somehow stayed unscathed", by working the varied line-lengths, unexpected line-endings, and mini sound riffs (the "ay" sound in the last line), against its prosaic qualities. Metaphors are mixed or only partially activated ("gifthorses", "unscathed"), but these infelicities are absorbed by a sense of an improvisational, thinking, pace. The shift by the time of *The Colour of Black & White* is essentially a thematic one, not one of technique, though there are some surprises – in particular the poem that writes the "same" childhood experience in Scots and then in English ("Kidspoem/ Bairnsang"). The focus is now on recalling the days of the 1950s and '60s, memoirs of Lochhead's mother and father and other people from that time, including herself, and, rather than girlfriend-boyfriend relationships, at the heart of the book are weddings and marriage (as with Verena in *Quelques Fleurs*). Like the new edition of *Dreaming Frankenstein*, this re-affirms Lochhead as a poet whose work is sociable and always intelligent.

RICHARD PRICE

Sing the demon blues

Barry MacSweeney, *Wolf Tongue,*
Bloodaxe, £12, ISBN 1852246669

What Barry MacSweeney wrote were not poems so much as sound sculptures; as in this passage from *The Book of Demons*, an account of the poet's struggle with alcoholism:

> This is the hell time of the final testament
> the ultimate booking, the whipped out ticket, little Hitler
> with Spitfire pencil on permanent jack-up; when he's not red
> carding
> your fanned-out fucked-up Bourneville chocolate cheekbones
> he's planning an invasion down your throat.
> Big Jack with the bad crack,
> just so peak and gleaming visor, ferret eyes
> glinty like fresh poured Tizer – the seepage of the coleslaw,
> the duff mayonnaise.

Voice was not something MacSweeney developed in laboratory-style workshop conditions, not something he polished and presented to cautious literary agents; in fact he frequently seems threatened by it. The chief demon appears as a

                                                              gem-hard
             hearted agent of my worst nightmare, this MC with spuriously
                    disguised gesture, this orchestrator of ultimate hatred,
                               the man with no eyes, no cranium, no brow no hair.
             He will always be known as the Demon with the Mouth of Rustling
                    Knives, and the meshing and unmeshing blades
                               are right in your face.

This demon is, amongst other things, a kind of poet, or at least a wielder of
language, whose mouth, unable to sing, has mutated into a pit of moving
blades.

    Wolf Tongue opens with some early lyrics, followed by MacSweeney's first
assured success: "The Last Bud", written in the long, flexible line of *Autumn
Journal*, or a Romantic conversation poem. The tone is steady, measured, and
capable of a disarming frankness:

>   I have only one half of my parenthood.
>   The other isn't dead, but he lingers on
>   this side of breath with the tenacity
>   of a rat. That breakdown in relations
>   doesn't even bother me now…

Tellingly, such candour already co-exists with a more theatrical mode of
expression. The poem signs off with a flourish as dramatic as Berryman's at
the end of *The Dream Songs*:

>   …wave your naked bodies
>   about like freedom flags. Ahead of me
>   is brilliant darkness, and the king
>   of night. This is a signed resignation;
>   I am finished with your kingdom of light.

    As John Wilkinson has commented, many of MacSweeney's finest poems
are found at the end of a period in his writing, when he has exhausted one
particular style or persona. "The Last Bud" is just such a farewell: to
mainstream literary society (MacSweeney's long exile began here, lasting until
the publication of *The Book of Demons*), but also to his own earlier poetic
practices: we will not find a single, stable speaking voice in MacSweeney's
poetry again until "Finnbar's Lament", twenty years later.

    In the interim, MacSweeney adopted a series of fractured, distorted
voices. In the poems of the 1970s and early '80s, MacSweeney's "voice" is to be

found somewhere in the shifts of register, the chasms which open up within the voice itself: "Just Twenty Two – And I Don't Mind Dying" (1971) is able to move between the faux-naïf "If finesse is crinkly you're a Dairy Box wrapper" (which sounds like a parody of his own earlier posturing) and "Wake up cunt you're living your life in bed" (perhaps the most bracing translation yet of Rilke's demand: "Du Musst dein Leben andern"). This edgy, aggressive voice finds its fullest expression in a work of the early '80s: "Jury Vet" is a long meditation on contemporary sexuality and the forces that would degrade desire to a branch of consumerism. MacSweeney enacts this process by marrying the breathless clichés of fashion magazines to just about every fetish and perversion you can name, facilitated as always by a Hopkinsesque knack for portmanteau words:

> take the mould, pube lichen, pistol come, quim
>   trigger fanny juice, dewy fern
>   hair swifted, sex weaponry
>   in her go root.
>
>
>   YOU THE SHIMMERTEXING PEARL
>   WITHOUTEN SPOT OR BODY BRUISE...
>
>   YOU MUST
>   teach me all there is to know
>   of
>   pinstripe boxjacket tuxedo woman's pillhat
>   velvet waistcoats,
>   &
>   Cup Court Shoes.

To paraphrase a line from Pasolino's film *Salo* (an apt enough frame of reference): "Taken to excess, everything is good". MacSweeney avoids didactic commentary or straightforward satire: the poem embraces the confused and confusing world of contemporary sexuality as much as it is repelled by it.

Ranter (1985), in contrast to the delirious excess of "Jury Vet", presents a pared-down, short line. This persona is not besieged by the demands of society the way the speaker of "Jury Vet" is: he is outside society altogether, likened to a reiver or beserker. The title-poem begins

> Ranter loping
> running retrieving
> motoring chasing

her with a cloakclasp
sniffing the trail
loving wanting
eyes on any horizon
but this blind spot
leaping the fence of his enclosure
nose down in open fields
stunned with blood
trailing her scent . . .

. . . and so on for forty pages, with barely a let-up in the urgency of the rhythms. *Ranter* is perhaps MacSweeney's most achieved work; with it he perfected what had always been his natural mode, the lament. All of his subsequent major works would be attempts to express some awesome, never-quite-defined loss. In "Finnbar's Lament", for instance, described by MacSweeney as *Ranter*'s "comet's tail", the persona he adopts is old, ancient. *The Seafarer* and *The Wanderer* loom large, finding the poet at his most lyrical:

Opening of her lids was like the rising of larks
in the blue slowness of a stubble-burning day.
She would stretch out her arms, disgrace-fetcher,
and I would lose my identity for hours on end . . .

"Finnbar's Lament" is one of the most beautiful poems in the language. A few readings secure its unique tone and atmosphere in the memory, and soon every line rings with a musical rightness:

My heart alone an instrument of shame.
Let go Siobhan
to wander back with friends…

We never had the ring of care
    beneath each eye.
She always had her things to do
and I had mine.

The inclusion of *The Book of Demons* (including the sequence called *Pearl*) brings us up to date. Pearl is the story of a mute girl whom MacSweeney taught to write, and if the demons personify a threatening, malevolent voice, then *Pearl* is their antithesis: a voice that barely exists, and must be nurtured and protected. Blake's *Songs of Innocence and Experience* is the model, and just as there is a darker aspect to the *Pearl* lyrics than first appears, so *The Book of Demons* contains a vulnerable, wounded side. In *Pearl*, we are back in the idyllic world of the first section of *Briggflatts*, tonally and geographically:

> Moon afloat, drunken opal shuggy boat
> in an ocean of planets and stars.
> Fierce clouds gather over me
> like a plaid shawl.
> Gone, gone, click of quarter irons
> to Nenthead, Alston and beyond.

Place-names in MacSweeney-territory carry enormous weight: throughout his writing we are returned to Allendale, Dirt Pot and Sparty Lea, and each time the place-names seem to acquire further resonance.

In *The Book of Demons*, the fractured personality has been cobbled together, a single persona with many names: Barry, Bar, the Pookah Swanne, Swanne Lud, etc. The demons likewise mutate into a variety of phantasmagoric horrors: they are the Stasi, the poet's father, even the doctors in the drying-out clinic where the poet was treated – but they are also part of the self-portrait. Alcoholics are capable of inflicting terrible hurt on their loved ones, and frequently live in terror of their own anger. One reading of the demons is that they are a paranoid projection of the poet's own capacity for harm and self-harm. The best of these late writings constitute some of his most powerful poetry: "Daddy Wants To Murder Me", "Sweeno, Sweeno", "Up A Height And Raining", "Strap Down In Snowville", "Tom In The Market Square Outside Boots", and "John Bunyan To Johnny Rotten" are set pieces within the work, MacSweeney's trademark hysterical verbosity put to the service of clear-eyed vision:

> O hello, Othello, black and green bastardo,
> please be Mr Stepaside. I've arrived.
> It is dark now and always dark.
> And demons will step from that darkness.
> I am the Pookah Swanne MacSweeney,
> wingflap homme man, jalousie
> my daily trade – my eternal war game
> against you and the world, drunken to the last, flung
> to the lost in the final Labour council-run
> public toilet on earth . . .

It would be a pity, however, if these late poems were seen to define MacSweeney. As Louis MacNeice put it, "the lyric is always dramatic". MacSweeney repeatedly reminds the reader of the artifice involved: in the above extract, "jealousy" is written "jalousie" (elsewhere, "stars" become "stares", and "sun" becomes "sunne"), recalling Chatterton's fraudulent Medieval poetry, which also made use of the estranging effect of idiosyncratic spelling and the use of a persona to enable a radical new poetry. Typically, though, MacSweeney had already moved on: at the time of his death, he was translating Apollinaire (a selection is to be published by Equipage), and *Wolf Tongue* ends with several previously uncollected poems, including "When the Lights Went Out a Cheer Rose in the Air", a final lament, this time for himself, written while MacSweeney was on the road (and back on the bottle), promoting *The Book of Demons*.

As Lowell said of Berryman, "he never stopped fighting and moving all his life; at first, expert and derivative, later full of output, more juice, more strange words on the page, more obscurity". Any one of the styles and personae he adopted could have brought MacSweeney fame, had he built a career on them; but he never allowed vision to decay into mannerism, pursuing each style only until he had mastered it, then moving on.

PAUL BATCHELOR

It will not be denied

Edwin Morgan, *Love and a Life: 50 Poems*,
Mariscat Press, £9, ISBN 094658835X

Most critical essays on Edwin Morgan begin with a survey of the diverse nature of his work. He is "sonneteer", "elegist", "translator", "playwright", ingenious discoverer and perpetrator of concrete and science fiction poems. Is there, then, a key to what Stuart Kelly has called the "mysteries of Morganism"? Some years ago, Christopher Whyte suggested that it lay "in the special status of his love poetry" and one might well argue that the multiple voices and styles adopted by Morgan are, in part, strategies of indirection forced out of him by the need to be circumspect about his homosexuality. Whyte's important essay developed two equally significant interviews he conducted with him in 1990, during the course of which Morgan spoke in detail about his life as a gay man and explicitly acknowledged the importance to his poetry of the '60s of the "link" between sexuality and creativity.

Love and a Life confirms the central place sexual and emotional relationships have played in Morgan's life, and suggests their importance to his poetry. "Love", he writes, "fills us and fuels us and fires us to create". It is "a probe" that galvanises us to explore a universe whose inexhaustible multiplicity is difficult to name, although with typical urgency Morgan tries: "the shoals the voids the belts the / zones the drags the flares it signals all to / leave all and to navigate" ("Love"). This poem, then, signals something of the collection's ambition. Although focused on the personal it takes the odd, humourous jaunt back into prehistory ("Jurassic"), out into Nature ("Crocodiles"), and revisits the passions of famous literary lovers such as Onegin's Tatyana, St John of the Cross, St Teresa of Avila, Titania and Bottom.

It begins, however, with a list of names: "Frank, Jean, Cosgrove, John, Malcolm, Mark – loves / of sixty years" and Morgan was clear in an interview with Phil Miller for *The Herald* (19 May, 2003) that it is the explicitly personal nature of the verse that is its distinguishing feature and another fresh departure for him as a poet: "In the past I couldn't name people. There were penalties for it in the past. It's a new kind of poetry for me". Such novelty demands a new form, or, rather, one which, in its deliberate mixture of prosiness and song-like cadence, seems to echo traditional, familiar patterns the poet has employed elsewhere. First used briefly in the recent *Cathures* (2002), each of the poems presents between fifteen and seventeen lines that depend strongly for their effect on the type of alliterative linkage much favoured by Morgan since his earliest days as a translator of Beowulf, and hammer away on one rhyme in Skeltonic fashion until near the end when a short, sometimes jaunty, couplet varies the music before returning us to the dominant *rime riche* of the final line. It is a form suited perhaps both to the insistent, nagging, involuntary return of the poet's memories as well as to his vigorous attempts to remember past loves and celebrate present ones.

The collection is given the coherence of a sequence, however, not simply by a shared form and theme but by the way Morgan allows the start of one poem to recall the close of the previous one, focusing sometimes on a specific word which is then redeployed in a different context. The effect is one of overlap, of one memory sparking another. The difficulty with this technique is that it can become predictable. Once it has been noticed you start to look out for it and the echo can sometimes seem forced. This echo effect works best here when it returns, unexpectedly, after a span of poems. Some of the pleasure of reading "Titania" – one of the strongest poems in the collection – comes from the way it implicitly picks up on the closing lines of the very first poem, "Those and These", where Morgan evokes his various friends and lovers

crowding around him "pinning me, pulling my ears". Similarly, it is the attention to microlinguistic effects of great subtlety as well as to the pacing of individual lines that impresses most. Here is the second half of "Freeze-Frame" which presents the collection as a whole as a series of photographic stills:

> "When my head was on your knees
> And your hand was on my head, did you think time would seize
> Head, hand, all, lock all away where there is no ring of keys – ?"
> I did not, oh I did not,
> But look what I have got,
> Frame of a moment made for friendless friendly time to freeze.

The slow tenderness of the gesture itself, and its simultaneous existence as mere memory, are perfectly acknowledged and rendered by unobtrusive repetition and the careful spacing of alliterative effects. And it is precisely because of the care accorded to the positions of "head" and "hand" in these lines that the repetition of the word "all" and the use of the exclamatory "oh" – which might otherwise read too rhetorically – are so beautiful and moving. The sequence of fricatives then deftly bears the poem off into the ether of memory, the sound satisfyingly confirming the ambiguities of its final line.

Similarly, "Late Day", which takes as its theme the commonplace of a gloomy winter day in Glasgow, derives only some of its pathos from our knowledge that the writer is old and suffering from cancer ("Scan Day"). Far more significant to the poem's success is the finely judged repetition of key words and the masterly way in which he allows internal rhyme to soften the expected blows of the end rhymes. Here is the second half of the poem:

> If darkness kept the world like a closed eye, we
> could only get our nightmare to search and gaze
> From its rolling red and bridled eyeball as we
> ride it down and down where muzzles never graze.
> How great the winter sun
> When horrors are undone
> By gentlest flimsiest fingers lighting our fingers
> as we open the curtains on a day content to
> glimmer and not to blaze.

The last three lines are tact incarnate, their movement exactly replicating the hesitant motion of fingers at curtains, at once apprehensive yet accepting of the slight grace conferred by winter sun.

The part of this sequence that works best is comprised of the poems that deal with the poet's cancer ("Scan Day", "Skeleton Day"), through to the lovely evocations of "Titania" and out into the four poems "Tatyana", "Teresa", "John (1)" and "John (2)". "Skeleton Day" is moving not simply because of its rueful picture of "the benedictions of the bone scan", but because Morgan allows memories and images from earlier poems in the sequence to flood the final lines in a quite unexpected way. "Skull, ribs, hips emerge / from the dark like a caravan / Bound for who knows where", and in those words we glimpse again fragments of Morgan's wartime service in the desert. This poem ends with an image of a frail but determined body "Still of a piece and still en route, beating / out the music of tongs and bones while / it can". A few poems later those "bones and tongs" return but now humourously, gently transformed into the music Bottom hears as he woos Titania.

"Titania" is a significant poem in Morgan's oeuvre in general because of the question it poses half way through. Ostensibly a question about Titania's and Bottom's ridiculous relationship, it may also be asked of the collection as a whole and how it stands in relation to all Morgan's previous love poetry: "So why is it touching?" In response, and with a critic's coldest eye, one might also ask "But is it sufficiently touching?" This is a question Christopher Whyte asked of Morgan's post-1990 love poetry, which he does not find as persuasive as the beleaguered, censored work of the 1960s and '70s, work which he reads with an acute and sympathetic eye. Because Morgan can now speak openly his love poetry is "less transgressive" except when he returns, as in "Persuasion" (from *Hold Hands among the Atoms*, 1991), to "the backcourts and dim woodlands" of furtive encounters. Whyte's argument develops points first made by Morgan himself in his interviews with Whyte, significantly entitled "Power from things not declared". "Creative activity of any kind", Morgan remarked, "is not hindered by pressures and difficulties and tensions". If Whyte and the younger Morgan are correct then where does this leave the frank and joyful poems of *Love and a Life*? Morgan is too good and too experienced a poet not to have asked himself this question. Indeed, he can be heard doing so in "Persuasion" where the answer he gives suggests that if "intelligence" and "faith" are sufficient then not only a happier life but good poetry should still be possible.

Nevertheless, there are moments in this collection when one gets the impression that Morgan feels such questions may be a little beside the point, or simply not important enough. Some of the poems sound as if they have been written quickly in the first flush of enthusiasm for a new love. There is awkwardness of which Morgan is surely aware and yet he has been content to leave it as it is because this collection is as much a testament to a life lived, to life and love in the process of living and loving, as it is a considered collection of verse. At least as worthy of consideration and attention as the "power" and "tension" of earlier lyrics is the "affection" ("Titania", "Harry") plainly and honestly celebrated in these poems. The aesthetic is quite different and reminds one of American examples such as O'Hara and Schuyler. And yet Morgan remains as astute as his best critics. For surely his poem "G" ingeniously dramatises the critical argument outlined above. Here is the furtive scene of tension: a married man speaking in broad Glaswegian, the vivid, transgressive detail of a blow-job. But then that scene is suspended as the withheld kiss is finally planted on the writer's lips "at Central Station", "in broad daylight":

> It will not be denied
> In this life. It is a flood-tide
> You may damn with all your language but it breaks
> and bullers through and blatters all platitudes
> and protestations before it, clean out of sight.

Is the kiss sexual, affectionate, both simultaneously? Is the rhetorical, triumphant close less powerful than the dramatic opening? There will be no shortage of readers, critics, and fans, maybe even the odd poet or two, eager to answer these questions.

DAVID KINLOCH

✿

You can't make an omelette

Marilyn Hacker, *Desesperanto*,
Norton, $23.95, ISBN 0393054187

These elaborately patterned poems of pain and longing resist any crude critical antithesis of high art versus raw experience or traditional form vs. contemporary feeling by being at once complex and seemingly easy. A strongly autobiographical poet who found her voice in the exhilarating moment of late '70s feminism, Marilyn Hacker has evolved a poetry of radical politics and openness to experience, in which both the dailiness of life and the experiencing female "I" are centrally present. Like Adrienne Rich or Audre Lorde, she makes her poetry constitute a record of her own life, her loves, her friends, her political beliefs; but unlike them, she lives as much in Paris as in New York and chooses to write with conversational freedom in the highly artificial forms of traditional European poetry. Because her voice

seems so natural and easy, the strictness of her metrical forms is unnoticeable at first glance, the poet wearing her mastery not as singing robes but a shirt and trousers, and not even those, perhaps, when she writes most nakedly. But these are not poems of lust and passion like her earlier *Love, Death and the Changing of the Seasons* (1990), for the poet's vulnerability now is towards betrayal and grief (many of the poems are elegies) which are intensified by her verbal artifice. Unexpectedly, perhaps, in formal poetry, one feels no tension between Hacker's conscious art and the raw experience encountered in, for instance, the "Migraine sonnets" linked by repeated last and first lines where the treadmill of grief grinds endlessly through sleepless nights:

> It's only half past two, you realize.
> Five windows are still lit across the street.
> You wonder: did you tell as many lies
> as it now appears were told to you ?
> And if you told them, how did you not know
> they were lies ? Did you know, and then forget ?
>
> There were lies. Did you know, and then forget
> if there was a lie in the peach orchard ? There was the lie
> a saxophone riffed on a storm-thick summer sky,
> there was the lie on a postcard, there was the lie thought
> and suggested....

These repetitive symmetries of traditional metre represent both an obsessive sorrow and the effort to curb it, the rhymes and repetitions seeming to come as uncontrollably as waves of pain. This kind of informally-formal poetry does carry a risk of chattiness; if the emotional temperature falls the conversational style can become prosaic and the clever repetitions boring. I found an occasional monotony in the sonnets of Parisian street life: good though they are on recording lively details – barges disappearing on a dirty canal the "color of piss and phlegm", long-legged black girls jumping double-dutch in the street, tourists gloved and scarfed for a chilly April – I wished that a poet so skilful with words might let them sing a bit more, as she does in "Crepuscule for Muriel", a poem that riffs on a single rhyme:

> instead of tannin seeping into the cracks
> of a pot, the void of an hour seeps out, infects
> the slit of a cut I haven't the wit to fix
> with a surgeon's needle threaded with fine gauge silk
> as a key would thread the cylinder of a lock.

Here the dance of the sound-pattern counteracts melancholy even when the subject is Muriel Rukeyser's aphasia – "she lost her words and how did she get them back / when the corridor of a day was a lurching deck?" Though the poem addresses loss, the result isn't emptiness but vivid, aching feeling. The pain and directness of the elegy for June Jordan have a similar strength:

> Whom do I address when I
> address you, larger than life as you
> always were, not alive now ?
> Words are not you, poems are not you,
> ashes on the Pacific
> tide, you least of all. I talk to my-
> self to keep the line open.

Another fine, deceptively simple poem, "English 182", describes teaching "American Women Poets of the Twentieth Century" to an unresponsive class. What at first looks like the usual teacher's gripe about students' ignorance ("We were a little vague on World War II. / We hadn't ever heard of Emmet Till"), turns painful and moving when it focuses on the one black girl who after a series of "scrupulous Bs" turns in a largely plagiarised paper and revenges herself for its low mark by

> glaring dully at me
> while I discussed black women's poetry
> refusing to make eye contact or speak
> as if her silence were an accident
> as if I didn't know what failure meant.

That resonant last line evokes several failures: the student's failure – trivial, but not to her – to sustain her B average, which is also the teacher's failure both to communicate with her class and to connect with the other outsider in it; the failure of a hoped-for alliance between the marginal groups represented by the lesbian teacher and her black student, which is also the failure of radical politics in the USA to deliver their promise; and most poignantly of all, though the student does not know it, the poet's bitter knowledge, attested by other poems in this collection, of the failure of love in her own life.

Love and loyalty fail, but Hacker's sensuality is still there for food: the brown loaf and the "blueberry jam that's almost black" in "Crepuscule for Muriel", the scent of bread across a street in the Paris sonnets, and above all the poem "Omelette", a *tour de force* of deceptive ease which interweaves sadness for lost friends and hopes with a deliciously Elizabeth David-sounding recipe for a mushroom omelette, all done in alcaics:

> First, chop an onion and sauté it separately
> in melted butter, unsalted, preferably.
> Add mushrooms (add girolles in autumn)
> Stir until golden and gently wilted.

Such omelettes were a feature of Hacker's youth, eaten with gay friends in New York as hangover cures in the '70s, or later over discussions of Emily Dickinson at a Parisian women's bookshop where "browned, molten gold ran on the platter: / a homely lyric", but the bookshop is now "another Left Bank restaurant" and nearly all the stylish "faggots (that's what they called themselves)" long dead of AIDS. Hacker's celebration of "Jamesian omelettes, skill and gesture" commemorates the pleasures it mourns, delicately sensual like the Platonic ideal omelette that "has only hot, loose egg at its heart, with fresh / herbs", where you sense the ghosts of sexy love-poems in that hot runny inside. The end of the poem gets as close as this book can to defying time: "Eat it with somebody you'll remember."

JANET MONTEFIORE

Poetry with drum & bass

Kwame Dawes, *New and Selected Poems, 1994–2002*,
Peepal Tree Press, £9.99, ISBN 1900715708

In what seems a very short time (his first book of poems was published only in 1994), Kwame Dawes has established a reputation as a poet and critic of an unusually wide-ranging and sympathetic intelligence. His biography demonstrates what a broad definition Caribbean poet can be: born in Ghana of West Indian parents, Dawes grew up in Jamaica, was educated in Canada, lives and works in the USA, and is mostly published in Britain. As a critic of contemporary Caribbean writing his analysis has been both generous and original, particularly in his work on the notion of a reggae aesthetic, as developed in his study *Natural Mysticism*, and illustrated both in his anthology *Wheel and Come Again* and his collection of poems *Shook Foil*. One has a sense, reading over Dawes's work, that his is an active intelligence in the best tradition of the practitioner-critic, the different facets of his work –

poetry, drama, public reading, reviewing, interviews with other Caribbean writers, and academic criticism – each serving to inform his overall artistic project.

It is clear from his account of the evolution of a reggae aesthetic that Dawes has a strong sense of the importance of tradition in understanding contemporary cultural expression, albeit that the tradition he identifies is not that Walcottian "mighty line of Milton and Marlow" which ratified the Caribbean canon. His exploration of the ways a complex reggae aesthetic, informed by a "history of rebellion and defiance" but characterised too by a Rastafarian re-definition of love, permeates and liberates the work of a whole generation of Caribbean writers (as well as a significant corpus of African, American, and European writers) fundamentally challenges prevailing orthodoxies but is argued with both authority and great subtlety. This is a period of redefinition for Caribbean culture and *Natural Mysticism* and *Wheel and Come Again* may well prove to be seminal texts in that process of reassessment and reclamation.

The notion of a reggae aesthetic – of the language moving to a different rhythm, under different kinds of pressure – also underpins all Dawes's work as poet. It is, in part, what has established the distinctive voice in his poetry, which is in other ways both formally and thematically diverse – ranging from the exploration of intensely private emotion to a consideration of huge public historical issues, particularly around slavery, the Middle Passage, and its consequences. But that history is, of course, itself one source of his private emotions; so again we have this sense of cross-over in Dawes's work, of the wholeness of his intellectual and artistic enterprise. The distinctiveness of the voice and the range of his concerns is perhaps best illustrated by reference to two of the eight collections represented in this generous *New and Selected Poems*; the 1996 collection *Requiem,* and the more recent *Shook Foil* (1998).

Requiem is a moving sequence of poems responding to the historical facts of the Middle Passage, powerfully evoking the horror of the slaves' experience but also managing to transcend the conventional responses of outrage and horror to convince his readers that the voices they hear, the emotions they encounter, are genuine, are felt. It is that conviction which enables the cathartic, healing energy of the sequence to come fully into play. The sequence is not just a re-imaging of the Atlantic crossing; it includes several poems that focus on the life-after-the-crossing, from those set in plantation times to others very much of the present. *Requiem* addresses the legacies of slavery with regard to issues of race and colour and confronts the notion of cultural alienation – even of the slaves and their descendants having in some neo-colonial sense connived with plantation lore in order to survive. The sequence is characterised by the economy of the writing, the sense of measured utterance, the *gravitas* and respect with which the poet addresses his subject. Not that these are in any sense decorous poems; the emotion that most informs them is an anger which – in the character of particular personae – is both raw and violent. As, for example, in the poem "Crime of Passion" which powerfully images both the rage of the man-who-would-become-the-slave and the frustration of alienation in his descendant who might-be-a-poet.

> . . . Oh to stay in the simple
> dialectic of hatred and brutality
> there at the edge of my flaming hut,
>
> to remain in that fire-bright place
> of purest hate, the stranger, a beast
> my fist clear-eyed, pounding life
>
> from his faceless howls. All this long before
> the gospel of crosses, blood; the song
> of promised lands I have embraced,
>
> long before I copulated
> with his books and gave birth to words,
> long before he found my tongue,
> could sing my tongue, owned my tongue
> while I toyed with his. Now my fist
> is a cataracted beast, unable to shake
>
> the monkey of affinity from my back.

The *Shook Foil* collection is in various ways a homage to Bob Marley which anticipates and complements Dawes's recent biography of the great Jamaican musician: it illustrates the formal awareness of the bass line that characterises the reggae aesthetic:

> .....the bass, a looping lanky
> dread, sloping like a lean-to
> defying gravity and still limping
> to a natural half-beat riddim,
> on the rain-slick avenue
> ("Some tentative definitions, 1")

Shook Foil also suggests the sensibility, the sensuality, the one-love weight of spirituality and metaphor – "light like a feather, heavy as lead" – that the reggae aesthetic encompasses:

> I stir from my trance hungry and thirsty,
>   and as sudden as a prayer formed, the sky is ashen –
>   heavy, sputtering pellets of rain.
>   I stand before the language of this storm
>   again an alien, a sojourner, waiting for a clue
>   to lead me homeward – a place of quiet rest.
>   ("I am a stranger on earth")

This is poetry dancing to a different drummer: the range of reference, the cultural assumptions bound into the poems, the cast and turn of the language, the lyrical drive . . . all of these announce another way of thinking about "poetry in English", where both "poetry" and "English" are problematic terms to be challenged and redefined.

And that's essentially what Dawes is doing through the rest of the *New and Selected Poems*, from the poems of alienation and lament in the Forward Prize-winning first collection *Resisting the Anomie*, through the extended verse narratives of *Prophets* and *Jacko Jackobus*, to the exploration of what it means to claim fully a New World African inheritance in his most recent collection *Midsummer*, which won the prestigious Hollis Summers poetry prize in the USA in 2001.

The new poems in this collection constitute a significant chunk of the book, and include several sharp and substantial pieces on coming to terms with middle age and trying to make sense of being who he is, now. I have perhaps made him seem too serious in this review, for there is much laughter in this book and a self-deprecating wit that can be disarming, as in "Fat Man":

> I stare at my stranger self in hotel mirrors.
> I am afraid to meet this stomach-glorious
> Creature, unable these days to find an angle
> Of satisfying grace. I am now a circle of errors.

STEWART BROWN

A world out of strange books

Gerrit Lansing, *A February Sheaf: Selected Writings, Verse and Prose.*
Pressed Water, $15, ISBN 0972108904
George Stanley, *A Tall Serious Girl: Selected Poems: 1957–2000*
ed. Kevin Davies and Larry Fagin, Qua Books, $25, ISBN 0970876327

Gerrit Lansing has published a selection from fifty years of his poetry and short essays, and titled it *A February Sheaf.* One might more reasonably expect a November or December sheaf from a poet born in 1928, as the ripe harvest of a life in poetry. But Lansing is specific: "A February Sheafe is not made up of Winter Words", he declares in his prelude, entwining this fair warning against Hardyesque summing-up with energetic epigraphs from the February section of Nicholas Breton's *Fantasticks* of c.1604. For this late book (one can't imagine it his last), which is a burst of amplitudes, not a record of diminishments, Lansing seizes Breton's sexy masculine sun as muse: "…now February, the Sun is gotten up a Cocke-stride of his climbing … the honour of Art is gotten by Exercise … the sap begins to rise up out of the root". As for William Carlos Williams, Lansing's season of choice, the source of his *ars poetica*, is Spring, early and cold; what he calls in the first poem a great "unsealing" where "shape is never still."

The book itself is restless in its three-part shape. First are nineteen "Poems Uncollected, Old and New", which, disconcertingly, seem not to be arranged from old to new or vice versa, although some are roughly datable from content. A perfectly formed, strange and sumptuous sonnet of "youthful homage to Stefan George" sits on the page facing a fragmentary, free-verse elegy, "blue, gay and mad", for the poet John Weiners, who died just last year. Not chronology, but surprise juxtaposition or free association seems to have inspired this gathering. There is a prose-poetry piece (the surreal parting of lovers in "Romanza"); there is a jumpy satiric riff on corrupted middle America called "The Wizard of Oz in the Blizzard of Oz"; there are wild, tumescent love poems. These outcroppings from published work, no less than the poetry in Part II (gleaned from three editions of *Heavenly Tree*), showcase Lansing's linguistic gifts. He has a deft, mischievous ways with allusion: he knows that with "kelson" comes all of Whitman's amativeness, with "tulgey" Lewis Carroll's rich, dark, and funny psychological landscapes, with "liquefaction" an entire renaissance of desire. He roots about in physics, biology, mathematics, and Hindu philosophy for vocabulary and metaphor. He casually places words which flirt with obscurity (funest, pleroma, tumulus, rhematic, swash, behovely, sigillary, pavan, volant). He will deliver the occasional flinty jewel of an epigram: "say not no to flow", "he can plant and he must plant", "Don't expect it [courage] where you look for it", "start because we were started / spinning tops of desire". Yet, *Heavenly Tree* (a life-long serial poem) reads as a complicated, many branched, deeply rooted hymn to amplitude. Lansing perceives in the world a gorgeous generosity of materiality, love, presence, growth, and the link of language to all of these:

> A WRIT is a route, a way and a map of a way . . . From the center of nothing something spreads out, that then there now. From zero jumps two, two being how something is apprehended. Only a stone's throw from writing to root. The rite of winter is the root of spring.

The book is ballasted at its end by a full eighty-three pages of "Reviews, Essays, Gists". "Gists" is a good word for them: their matter is quickly and intelligently rendered. One finds Lansing's poetic credo (and cosmic viewpoint) stated backwardly in a negative critique of Tom Clark's biography of Charles Olson, which he deems to be marred by "the rhetoric of belittlement, disparagement, meiosis". His own assessments are anything but meiotic. He reads appreciatively the work of poets and artists, friends and forebears, some, like him, lucky enough to have escaped the mill of mainstream attention. "The School of Boston, in poetry", he announces, "middle this century, is an occult school, unknown". Among his confreres, Lansing turns his loving laser-light toward Stephen Jonas, Thorpe Feidt, Clark Coolidge, John Clarke, Robin Blaser, Robert Duncan. From the short-lived literary magazine *SET* (1961–4) he excerpts his "hortatory" intentions for American poetry at that volatile time, and he pulls from his reading a personal canon made up of the famous, the neglected ("These States know how to Neglect"), the elusive, and those lost in translation. Thoreau, Gérard de Nerval, Frederick Goddard Tuckerman, Oscar Vladislas de Lubicz Milosz, Jean Baudrillard, Aleister Crowley: one wonders what occasions inspired these disparate tributes, at once gnomic and brash. "The Neptunian Character", and "La p(l)age poétique", bristling statements of poetics, perform what they proclaim: the "figurative beach or page [as a] head for launching or welcoming down the grand insolite poems to come".

George Stanley (b. 1934) has also been selecting from his life's work for publication in 2003 with the help of two editors, Kevin Davies and Larry Fagin, who write an informative prefatory note to *A Tall, Serious Girl: Selected Poems: 1957–2000*. Stanley spent his formative years in San Francisco, absorbing the west-coast version of the Olson/Duncan/Spicer atmosphere, the commitments to open-field poetics and to gay eroticism. His book is arranged chronologically and also geographically, tracing Stanley's passage in time and space from San Francisco, to New York, and Vancouver, and lastly to his outpost and home, Terrace, British Columbia, with trips to and in his ancestral Ireland an essential element of the mix. "Stanley is an American-Canadian-Irish poet" his editors claim: yet this doubly-hyphenated identity is both Stanley's poetic motherlode and also accounts for his having "disappeared from American literary surveillance", which doesn't reach all the way to Terrace and, except for a notorious few, is uninterested in following poets beyond the moment when their youth, energy, and sheer presence fueled some voluble, "gang-minded" (the phrase is Duncan's) avant-garde, intent on revolutionizing the word.

The first poems in the volume ride the waves of that high-energy youth. Stanley's prose poetry rampage of American "Westron" myth, "Tete Rouge", sets loose a wild red-headed Scotsman who shoots bald eagles, can't mount a horse, and "drinks, and dances, and sings", in a hilarious deconstruction of traditional "winning of the west" narratives. A companion piece, "Pony Express Riders", is, by contrast, an elegiac tribute to "the men that fought and loved each other", full of haunting images of beautiful men riding through shifting light-filled landscapes. A long poem, "Phaedus", is a veritable symphony of eros and anxiety, shot through with the imagery of trains and horses.

But the volume deepens as it proceeds away from San Francisco, risking the "mountains and air" of British Columbia. From there the poet portrays himself "build[ing] up a world out of strange books", and "learning to live alone, learning alone / to live? In Terrace?" Stanley becomes an able, albeit often reluctant, chronicler of that deliciously absurd stage of human life: middle age. The dominant tone of half of the book is a near-perfect blend of depression and comedy, as if to ask how the great jokes of mortality, loneliness, and marginality came to be played on George Stanley. "There will be more hangovers", he writes:

> The days that danced once
> are prisoners, of the years
>
> The seasons shock us
> w
> unbidden power, & we drink
> when it thunders …
>
> we feel spoken to & drink.

A long prose poem about being unable to write a long prose poem interrupts itself to say "This is not poetry. But what would a poem about Terrace be like?" Stanley's poems enclose their own distress about their author's aging body and soul, and about "the huge surrounding fucked reality", that is North American life somehow carried on amid advertisements and "cars, cars, & carts & such", "placidity and obesity", the "two-stage foulness" of flat, chemical drinking water, the "stunned faces – the stalled lives". More our world than the wild, lost poetic 1950s, whether in San Francisco, Boston, or New York, is this "nowhere", where he has nonetheless created something of "a good self / but off the road, a limbless self, good wood, no knots / … a pole". Indeed, by the last poem, the mysterious "tall, serious girl" makes her appearance as Stanley himself, fluidly re-imagined in all his roles as son, lover, mother, father, traveler, "old man", and poet.

SARA LUNDQUIST

◢

The Silence Artist

Avraham Ben Yitzhak, *Collected Poems (translated by Peter Cole)*
Ibis Editions (Israel), $13.95, ISBN 9659012497

Avraham Ben Yitzhak is a poet whose achievement consists, in large part, of the refusal to write poetry. He was born Abraham Sonne in 1883 in the city of Przemsyl in Galicia (now Poland). His hometown had once been famous for wonder-working Hassidic rabbis who were skilled at exorcising dybbuks, but by his time the Jews were mostly religious rationalists, and he received a sober traditional education. He moved to Vienna, where he was wont to sit in literary cafes, in silence. Influenced by Rilke, he considered writing in German. Instead, an active Zionist, he committed himself to Hebrew. Eleven exquisite lyrics published in small magazines between 1903 and 1928 make up his entire *oeuvre*. In 1938 he fled to Palestine as a refugee, where he wrote nothing, and died of tuberculosis in 1950.

All of his poems are about the yearning for renunciation. They are written in a refined, quasi-Biblical Hebrew. His earliest published poem, "Bright Winter" ends:

And it seems:
together with the planet's heart,
my heart inside me pulses;
and with the current it flows
as they stream beneath the crust of ice.
Pure ... the world ...
is pure ...

And from his final poem, "Blessed Are They Who Sow And Do Not Reap":

Blessed are these
for they will be gathered to the heart of the world
    wrapped in the mantle of oblivion
– their destiny's offering unuttered to the end.

He was admired by Arnold Schoenberg, Robert Musil, and above all by
Elias Canetti, who entitled a chapter of his memoirs "Sonne": the poet was
described as "the one perfect man in Vienna". Ben Yitzhak was physically
striking – tall, very thin, with blue eyes recessed behind thick pince-nez. When
he chose, which was seldom, he spoke German with extreme eloquence. The
joke that was told about him was that he would be contributing to a discussion
by saying nothing, and his interlocutor would respond, "Nu, now let's be silent
about something else?"

In Israel – despite or because of his non-production – he acquired a
reputation as a poet's poet. His terse formality was seen as a corrective to the
verbose romanticism of other poets of his generation. After his death his
collected work was published in book form, in an edition of 400 copies.

Surely Ben Yitzhak was invented by the same God who composed Kafka.
Both of them were Jews born in outlying provinces of the Austro-Hungarian
Empire, both masters of the German language, both Zionists who taught
themselves Hebrew and dreamed of living in Palestine, both writers who
doubted themselves obsessively and were tempted to destroy their own
work; and both of them passed away from the same disease. Ben Yitzhak was a
Silence Artist – yet perhaps (to adapt a sentence from Kafka) The Silence
Artist was not really Silent at all; he would have scribbled away like anyone
else, if only he could have found something worth writing.

Ben Yitzhak has retained a small but avid following (as a search on the
Internet will reveal). And at last his work has come out in English, in a
parallel-text translation by Peter Cole, which accurately captures the poet's
lyrical stiffness, and the ambiguity of his intentions. The book is thoroughly
footnoted, and contains an informative postscript by Hannan Hever detailing

Ben Yitzhak's life and works. It is published by Ibis Press (www.ibispress.com) – an excellent Jerusalem-based outfit which specialises in literature from the Levant: mostly translations into English from Hebrew and Arabic. All of their publications are elegantly printed and worth investigating.

JONATHAN TREITEL

❧

More lite than light

Hans-Magnus Enzensberger, *Lighter Than Air: Moral Poems*
(translated by David Constantine), Bloodaxe, £8.95, ISBN 1852245808

The dust-jacket of *Lighter Than Air* tells us that Hans Magnus Enzensberger (b. 1929) is "the most important German poet" and that "No British poet can match him in his range of interests and his moral passion". This is just terrible rubbish: it's like a script for Radio Baghdad or something. Enzensberger is three years older than Adrian Mitchell, and pretty similar as a poet. His work isn't passionate at all; it's both ironic and flatteningly simplistic. It used to be that people went to poetry for refuge from the crassness and deceit of the commercial speech around them: but this blurb is language weaponised to neutralise your brain at the point of sale. No one in their right senses would read Enzensberger if they could be reading Mayröcker, Huchel, Eich, Arendt, Jandl, Heissenbüttel, Becker, Kling, or Draesner.

The terror of German poets is that they are going to be didactic, or moralising, or authoritarian, or that they are going to engage in supersensitive self-comforting anxiety about the Decline of the West, or that they are going to revert to *nouveau riche* type and produce something monumental in bulk and without quality. Enzensberger achieves all these goals, although he sometimes has to sneak up on them. Even in the 1959 anthology *Expeditionen*, when he was young, he was one of the less interesting poets in the book. The 1950s were a golden age of German poetry: and Enzensberger's anti-aesthetic, authoritative, civic simplifications did a great deal to hasten its end. His contemporary Peter Rühmkorf (with *Volksvermögen*) and he (with *Allerleirauh*) both edited anthologies of children's poetry – as a protest against the subjective dizziness and complexity of learned German poetry. The link with children's writing is that Enzensberger wants to supervise paternalistic politicians in a paternalist way. Enzensberger's closeness to the surface of politics and the media means that his poetry has banality as its content – and the ironic twist is always too predictable. Folk wisdom is hoarily akin to folk stupidity.

To write so simply – like Brecht, like Prévert, like Arp – was revolutionary, in 1960. Enzensberger benefited from the Brecht aura. To be a Brecht pupil, however, you have to be a Brecht scholar; Peter Hacks and Heiner Müller (among others) are real pupils. Enzensberger said, back then, that he preferred a railway timetable to a poem – because it was more precise. This appealed both to insecure poets and to poetry-hating journalists. Enzensberger was the public face of poetry because he was as indifferent to quality as journalists are. As a citizen, Enzensberger was probably right about the public life of the Bundesrepublik, most of the time – and he is a brilliant media critic. As a poet, he was a good committee member and leader of team-building exercises. In the 1970s, he began to criticise political engagement, and accrued enormous prestige for this, but went on writing in exactly the same way.

He has written a lot of poems about science. The one about Johnny von Neumann, here, tells us what he looked like but not that he invented the computer program. Is this history of science for non-scientists, or poetry without science, without history, and with a Big Plain Moral? The frames around his coloured pictures of moralised reality suggest how reality is excluded from thought; what is inside the frames is stock footage.

What is enjoyable in his work is the lightness of touch – unlike some writers of slimline talent, he never tries too hard. The title comes from a not at all bad, charming, poem:

> Lightest of all of course
> like forgotten grief
> and the smoke of the definitely last cigarette
> is the first person
>
> (...)
> Least of all perhaps
> weighs what remains of us
> when we are under the ground.

Its argument is entirely prefigured in a poem by Francis Quarles (1592–1644):

> My soul, what's lighter than a feather? Wind.
> Than wind? the fire. And what, than fire? The mind.

What's lighter than the mind? A thought. Than thought?
This bubble world. What than the bubble? Naught.

Not only does Quarles leave Enzensberger standing as a poet, but the topos is rather more battered and tattered than it was 350 years ago. Quarles was rather a hack, and knocked out hundreds of Emblems of similar tone and rhythmic patterns. Maybe this link to the didactic Protestant piety and diligence of the seventeenth-century reveals the overall method of Enzensberger's poetic works, and his peculiar virtues.

ANDREW DUNCAN

Exchange rates

Monica Youn, *Barter*,
Graywolf, US $14.00, ISBN 1555973817

Monica Youn's *Barter* repeatedly reminds its reader that, by nature, perception is multiply mediated: always by the viewer's perspective and language, at times also through myth, painting, environment, and others' consciousnesses. As the speaker investigates the influence of electronics on cognition ("Electronica"), or intense heat helps her to discern her relationships to physical touch and metaphysical belief ("A Parking Lot in West Houston"), the poems often position her in a negotiation between tenor and vehicle in order to understand both better; it is to these transactions that the word "barter" strangely and suitably applies. Although the title may suggest that the poems reduce these transactions to clear-cut exchanges, that is anything but the case. Youn's taut lines, linguistic precision, measured rhythms, and exacting syntactical structures inform, both deftly and intelligently, her poems' deliberations on the problems of perception and knowledge.

A studied maturity, then, already differentiates *Barter* from the majority of first collections. *Barter* is also distinguished by its particular variety of poetic styles, which says something of the rising generation of US poets as well as of the present moment in US poetry. Over the last decade or so the dominant schools of US poetry – neo-formalism, Language and post-Language poetries, and mainstream personal narrative – have all gained greater exposure through university writing programs, anthologies, print and online journals, writing centres, etc. In turn, this pervasive dissemination has put poets in the States into regular contact with a wider range of poetries than ever before. This development means multiple, more varied traditions influence newer poets' work, as the greater visibility of "experimental" poetry in particular opens up new territory in a way we see far less of in the UK. In *Barter*, while poems such as "Three Generations after Larkin" and "Décor" operate in an essentially linear, personal narrative mode, "Drawing for Absolute Beginners" and "Verandah", with their topically and stylistically disparate sections, resist narrative in the creation of inexplicit, vivid, and resonant accumulations. Other poems move between these artificial poles, evincing trajectories that build impressionistically, as in "Alaska Airlines".

As a result of the collection's sense that we apprehend nothing directly, many of the poems in *Barter* appear as individual acts of alienated spectatorship. In such a position, the speaker often manifests a tension between controlled detachment and an earnest desire for human contact. In "Letter from Contra Costa", for instance, the speaker addresses a you "drifting away from me", such that the addressee's face is "already [. . .] / rinsed of detail, the inside of an elbow". Studying that blankness, the speaker cannot decide which definition of marmoreal applies to it: has the addressee become simply "*Marmoreal* meaning white like marble or *marmoreal* / meaning white and hard like marble"? The speaker's inability to ascertain and thereby fix the meaning of what she sees renders her powerless. Consequently, the steady, distinct observations that compose the first five stanzas break down in the last, as the speaker relates, "I walked // for three hours won't you make the poem Christmas, / the answer to everyone's question, greek fire?" The plea for the addressee to decide positively "everyone's question" – what is our real relation to one another – is a plea for the Promethean gift of enlightenment. The addressee's answer would be a kind of Christmas for the speaker, as her painful, itinerant uncertainty could not only come to an end, but would also place her in the relation to the addressee that she so desires.

Other poems in *Barter* also correlate linguistic with emotional control. In "Polaroid", the speaker handles a disconcerting event – the appearance of a pornographic photograph on her windshield – by considering the picture in parts. In the first three sections of the poem, the speaker describes different areas of the picture – left, top left, and lower right – and thereby appropriates the photograph through the poem's language and structure. These multiple perspectives seem to give her insight into the photographer, such that the fourth and final section builds on the study of the photo with a contemplation of its taker's motive. Here is that section in full:

Such effort,
young one,

and to what end?
To locate appetite

that would be as
maple in the

mouth? To use
your own hand

to mark the line
between that

darkness and the
encroaching dark?

Foregrounding the ways of seeing that blur or "mark the line / between" the darkness we know and the "encroaching dark" beyond, *Barter* ultimately places us between them. It is a book at once disturbing, elegant, and faithful.

CARRIE ETTER

*

Poetry Chronicle

Rhian Gallagher, *Salt Water Creek*, Enitharmon, £7.95, ISBN 1900564386,
Martha Kapos, *My Nights in Cupid's Palace*, Enitharmon, £7.95,
ISBN 1900564432, Frances Williams, *The Red Rubber Ball of Happiness*,
Seren, £6.95, ISBN 1854113364, Julia Copus, *In Defence of Adultery*,
Bloodaxe, £7.95, ISBN 1852246073, Tim Liardet, *To the God of Rain*,
Seren, £6.95, ISBN 1854113356

So many writers, it seems, are after the poetry of everyday life. Unfortunately, the average poet's daily thoughts are about as boring as a reality TV show, only more pretentious. (Bus stop epiphanies and walks in the park abound.) Whatever happened to imagination, drama, attitude? New Zealand-born Rhian Gallagher's first collection may be short on drama, with its hometown landscapes and scenic bike rides, but her deceptively matter-of-fact voice doesn't lack for attitude. In the ironically titled "Find a Partner" (Gallagher is gay), she evokes the awkwardness of puberty with a few crisp stanzas on school dancing lessons. "[A] rise and a fall and a boy / with a grip on my arm as if it were a baseball bat. / The feeling of being inside my body / arrives with this news – it's going to be difficult." Elsewhere the poet, who lives in London, recounts a rare visit from her brothers without sentimentality, leaving her emotions to be read between the lines. (Tact is one of Gallagher's great strengths.) The piece closes with a movingly understated scene of their daytrip to Hove:

> . . . [T]he car goes ropy, and we know
> if we stop the whole thing will likely die –
> as if this is where the family's always been as we sing,
> sing like hell for all the lights to turn green.

Gallagher's spare but musical language catches just the right details of a setting (walking past a Chinese laundry, she hears "the sound of a press / squeezing a line along a sleeve") and occasionally blossoms into a quiet lyricism. Describing the impact of her mother's death on her siblings, she notes, "It's like nowhere when the grief finds them, / . . . [m]y older brother swimming out beyond the raft / in the dead of winter, swimming against nothing, against the gap."

While grounded in ordinary experience, Martha Kapos' fertile imagination tinges everything with surrealism – in the space of a single poem, she likens a person's hand to a small sun, a sickle, a fruit, a star and (most bizarre) a parking space. An unusually accomplished debut, *My Nights in Cupid's Palace* displays a strong ear for rhythm and tonal control, yet the associative fuzziness of her writing eventually grows tiresome. "The *A to Z* of your smile without / getting lost" counts as a complete sentence in Kaposspeak – though at least the metaphor generates a delicious resolution when she looks "it up [the smile, presumably] / in the index under S":

> Something Circus
> Something Crescent
> Something Close.

That Kapos is usually close to meaning something, no matter how convoluted the path by which she arrives there, saves her work from being totally incomprehensible. Her vagueness of reference is a technique familiar from contemporary American poetry, a way of gesturing at complex, fleeting emotional states through a suitably fluid language. Recalling the taste of a blackberry (which in turn seems to be a metaphor for her lover's smile) she writes, "Hard losing itself / in soft, fusty and sweet, like hearing / your own voice all wrong." I'd be hard-pressed to explicate that literally, but I get it – which is the point when reading these oblique lyrics. Kapos successfully balances mystery with a linear narrative in the more straightforward piece "Wolf" (though I'm still not sure whether the animal who materialises in her kitchen is actually a wolf, a skittish pet dog, or an angry partner):

> Please come and let me feed you.
> I hold out my hand
> like a beggar and you are released.
> It is the deep red time of the body,
> I offer it as meat.

If anything, a bit of mystery would be welcome from Frances Williams, whose third book largely relies on vignettes about commonplace events: a cab ride, the weekly rubbish collection. Given such material, she can tend to end her poems not with a bang but a whimper, some forced note of catharsis. In "The Flats", passers-by gather to watch a building being demolished, then "walk out / Of the moment, / Inhaling its musk, / Fond and secret agents now / Of an ongoing dispersal."

Williams injects the better pieces with tension or menace, like the subtle unease that pervades "Letter From the Lake House": "I find / Myself in the sulky faces of the China cats. / The dance of the jam jars. / A morse of lit and unlit lamps." In "Diva" she imagines a retired opera star listening to a CD recorded in her prime. "The flat disc glitters in my hand. / I hear myself travelling / In two directions at once." (A nicely sketched portrait of pride and regret, the monologue also features the wicked enjambement "In the last act of my / Difficult Tosca.")

With its sophisticated conceits and formal variety, Julia Copus' second collection stands out from the norm. Divided into two parts – "Fission and Fusion" and "Astronomy and Perception", with epigraphs by scientists such as Stephen Hawking – the book wears its learning lightly. A piece titled "Forgiveness" (in physics the word refers to the "fracture toughness" of substances) applies the term to relationships, while the prose poem "Home Physics" borrows the language of classroom experiments to slyly portray a rocky romance – "ball bounces off end of stroked rod", "sledge hammer hits large mass resting on person", or my own favourite, "phantom bouquet". And in a dazzling elegy for her dead cousin, Copus gives us the first twenty lines of a poem, then repeats them in reverse order, so that they still make sense but say something different.

Despite these attractive trappings, Copus often resorts to generalising about human nature, adopting the universal "we" for a specious profundity. "It is down to us / whether we wait for things to pass / or manage, with a simple gesture, / to . . . set sail – / vessels of the possible" smacks of a New Age greeting card; love "gives and gives", "making us whole". She likes dispensing nuggets of wisdom in the second-person plural, too, as in "A Short History of Desire", which urges us to wake up and embrace life. "However deep asleep you think you are, / there always will be days like this – / a light, hair-tousling breeze and a sun that streams / into the dusty parlour of your heart." I say, keep on snoring.

Does the world really need more travel poems about Paris? Tim Liardet's latest volume contains several of them, plus a few verse snapshots of Florence for good measure. Other pieces dwell at length on mundane matters like the discovery of a "Wasps' Nest" under the floorboards in his lounge. "I stepped into the rug's radiance where / the great bay printed its shape / and I sensed the nest massage the soles of my bare feet like a jacuzzi of fire." Pass over these bloated, po-faced meditations and read his sequence of superb love poems instead. This account of a doomed affair, in 14-line episodes that loosely resemble sonnets, marks a sharp break from the rest of Liardet's work. "Look," he writes, "the old world snaps like a wishbone." Certain phrases recur from poem to poem – "[Y]ou are leaving. The train approaches. Things start to shake" – each time slightly altered, as if the same event were being seen from multiple angles. (The book's cover illustration and epigraphs are by the Futurist painter Boccioni.) The brevity of Liardet's chosen form forces him to pare the story down to its most essential details: his lover's wristwatch, her going-away coat, "the filament in the bulb". As he counts down the time they have left together, "the number of hours and of minutes rattle over at speed / like the destinations on the departure board". And when the end finally comes, he wakes up –

> . . . to find your eyes already open,
> shoes on, your coat round your shoulders
> or the weight of it off them, already slipping.
> The bird in the belly is crashing and flapping.

JANE YEH

The poet in the kitchen

Louis Zukofsky, *A Useful Art: Essays and Radio Scripts on American Design*, Wesleyan University Press, ISBN 0819566403

"The first casting in the colonies is said to have been a small iron kettle, made at Saugus probably about 1645, for 'The Company of Undertakers for the Iron Works.'" Louis Zukofsky doesn't say so – he doesn't have to – in his discussion of Ironwork in *A Useful Art*, but it can clearly be supposed that before 1645, when the good people of Saugus sat down to have tea – the colonists, that is, not the native Americans – the kettle they used was an import from the old country. Saugus (then Hammersmith), Massachusetts, was among the first iron works in colonial America. In 1642, Thomas Dexter of the Massachusetts Bay Colony sent bog-ore he had discovered in the Bay area back to England to establish if it might be successfully refined. It was: "The Company of Undertakers for the Iron Works" was established, and two years after that the Massachusetts General Court granted a charter for the production of iron. A year later, New England had its first "home-made" kettle. Much depends, Louis Zukofsky would clearly have us believe, on that first casting: "a small iron kettle, made at Saugus probably about 1645".

A Useful Art is the sixth volume of the Wesleyan University Press Centennial Edition of the *Complete Critical Writings of Louis Zukofsky*. It collects the essays and radio scripts the poet wrote while working on The Index of American Design for the Federal Arts Project, a division of the Work Projects Administration. Like all such New Deal initiatives, the purpose of The Index of American Design was to provide socially useful employment. It was to constitute a comprehensive history of American craft traditions at a time when such traditions were becoming finally obsolete as a means of production. This obsolescence, effected by that more vigorous of American traditions rampant industrialism, was the cause of considerable regret to a culture that was, in some respects, just becoming properly conscious of itself. As a result, and as a way of putting otherwise struggling writers to work, The Index of American Design was conceived: watercolours of design objects (eventually totaling some 18,000) to be supported by historically detailed textual accounts.

Judging by the essays and radio scripts which make up *A Useful Art*, Zukofksy wasn't just grateful for the work on the Index – he loved it. Here, then, is the poet, in the eighteenth-century American kitchen:

The utensils for preparing food are so many and their functions so varied that it is often hard to find a category for each separate implement. Considering various collections, the eye is impressed by their miscellaneousness. The names identify the uses: sugar-loaf cutter; cooker for small game; toasting fork; iron trivet for roasting birds; charcoal broiler with hinged lid; grooved boiler for collecting juices; skewer holder; grater; saltbox; noggin; mechanical bellows; plate warmer; mixing bowl; corn sheller; and flour sifter.

The pleasure of *A Useful Art* is very largely in such taxonomies. (A noggin, by the way, is a small mug). So here is Zukofsky in the same kitchen, this time noting all the activities that were performed there:

Cooking, baking, heating, lighting, dairying, laundering, carving, dyeing, spinning, weaving, and preparing remedies for the sick ... [The kitchen] required utensils for all of these processes – iron implements forged and cast by the country blacksmith, tin and brittania ware sold by travelling artisans and growing urban establishments, wares of wood, brass, copper, pewter, silver, pottery and glass.

From this, of course, Zukofksy can sometimes sound like a man who has not, well, spent quite as much time in the kitchen as he might have ("Really, I had no idea!"). Except that it is by no means only domestic objects that catch his eye. Here he is in one of the broadcasts that emerged from his research, a talk, in the form of an interview, on the history of the American lantern.

Int.: – Yes, but what or who were the Wide Awakes?
Mr.Z.: They were an outgrowth of the abolition movement. On Feb.25, 1860, Cassisus M. Clay, noted abolitionist from the South came to Hartford, Conn., to spur the Republicans to greater efforts for the cause. He was greeted by a torchlight parade of young party members – their lanterns gay and their torches flaming. But they were careful enough to wear caps and long black capes of oil cloth to protect their heads and clothes from the dripping oil.

A Useful Art is full of this stuff, is full of stuff in general; taxonomies of stuff, meticulous descriptions of stuff; compelling, erudite historical contextualizations of the things which made the fabric of pre-industrial American life. The book is the work of a poet who relished his day-job. It is also, very deliberately, a contribution to a home-grown literary tradition.

In *Call Me Ishmael*, Charles Olson's brilliant, eccentric critical response to *Moby-Dick* (published in 1947 but researched in the 1930s, and therefore of a moment with the writings of *A Useful Art*), it was very largely in terms of facts that Olson presented the novel to an audience he considered were not fully appreciating Melville's masterpiece. So,

> Economic historians, lubbers, fail to heft the industry in American economic life up to the Civil War. (In 1859 petroleum was discovered in Pennsylvania. Kerosene, petroleum, and paraffin began rapidly to replace whale oil, sperm oil, and spermaceti wax as illuminating oil, lubricants, and raw materials for candles.)

Before 1859, in other words, when Americans wanted to illuminate and lubricate, it was with whale oil, and sperm whale oil in particular, that they did so, hence the fact that, as Olson says,

> by 1830, 70,000 persons and $70,000 were tied up in whaling and such associated crafts as shipbuilding, sail lofts, smiths to make toggle irons, the thieving outfitters, their agents and the whores of the ports like New Bedford.

This level of investment in the whaling industry is set against the facts of pay and conditions: "During the 1840s and '50s it cost the owners 15¢ to 30¢ a day to feed each crew member." The consequence: "By the 1840s the crews were the bottom dogs of all nations and all races. Of the 18,000 men one-half ranked as green hands and more than two-thirds deserted every voyage."

The factuality of *Call Me Ishmael* was both critically appropriate and acutely contemporary, and, like Zukofsky's research, was a highly self-conscious move in a tradition which found poetry in the body of prose. Critically appropriate because the full richness of *Moby-Dick* is to be found in its handling of facts. Really to relish *Moby-Dick*, in other words, you to have to want to know about, The Line, The Dart, Cutting In, Cisterns and Buckets, The Try-Works. Nor was Melville alone among his contemporaries in wanting to present the circumstances of production. Really to enjoy *Walden*, for instance, you have to want to know, as Thoreau wants to tell you, that in making the hut in which he wrote his great book, he made use of the following items purchased at the following costs:

Boards, ...	$ 8 03½,	mostly shanty boards.
Refuse shingles for roof and sides, ...	4 00	
Laths, ...	1 25	
Two second-hand windows with glass, ...	2 43	
One thousand old brick, .	4 00	
Two casks of lime, . . .	2 40	That was high.
Hair, ...	0 31	More than I needed.
Mantle-tree iron, ...	0 15	
Nails, ...	3 90	
Hinges and screws, . . .	0 14	
Latch, ...	0 10	
Chalk, ...	0 01	
Transportation, ...	1 40	} I carried a good part on my back.
In all,	$ 28 12½	

What Melville and Thoreau want the reader to be interested in his how things are made, where "things" includes books, and where books are considered not only as the products of words and ideas, but as the outgrowth of a whole set of circumstances of production which go to make the writing life possible. From this point of view, then, a certain and very invigorating strain of American literature gains its purpose and its value from an attention to things; to the things and the processes which constitute the collective life out of which the literature emerges; or, as Zukofsky liked to think of it, to "objects".

Zukofsky coined the term "objectivism" when introducing an anthology of mostly young American poets in 1931. The young poets were Zukofsky himself, George Oppen, Charles Reznikoff and Carl Rakosi. (Muriel Rukeyser and Lorine Niedecker, who were to become closely associated with the group, were not included at this point.) In the anthology, these hitherto unknown poets were presented alongside the writers they took as their most important recent forbears, William Carlos Williams and Ezra Pound. Pound, in particular, was important to Zukofsky, who, alongside Basil Bunting, is the dedicatee of Pound's book *A Guide to Kulchur*; a fellow "struggler in the desert", as Pound's dedication somewhat melodramatically puts it. Always deeply committed to the sense of the poet as craftsman, hence his very deliberate sense of the poetic apprenticeship, Pound came to want a poetry of things. Thoreau's table of materials, in form and content, can read like a prototype for the baggier Cantos, where what is largely at issue is the bric-a-brac involved in the making of the poem. Among the ways Zukofsky differs from Pound, is in a more local, arguably more parochial, even culturally chauvinistic, sense of the kinds of thing an American poem should incorporate; and in a more carefully considered, even systematic sense of the processes involved in the making of things. Both of these aspects of his poetry can be found evolving in *A Useful Art*, and both take us back to the kettle.

One way of reading this book, one way Zukofsky allows it to be read, is as a story of the emergence of American cultural independence, as a history, through objects, of the making of a nation. That first casting, "the small iron kettle", is an early move in that story. And then look, Zukofsky tells us excitedly, how only a century or so later, the kettle has become a whole kitchen, and the kitchen is full, with its toasting fork, trivet, charcoal broiler, grooved broiler, "skewer holder; grater; saltbox; noggin". Here are the tropes of American abundance and Yankee adaptability in one sentence. Yankee taste, also, is noted and admired. Hence his comment on American tole- (table-) ware. "The japanning", he says, unapologetically,

> was often thin, and the decoration which would have seemed garish to the European connoisseur, was usually a matter of bold designs done in bright colours. But this toleware was exceedingly popular with country people and the Yankee pedlar fostered its distribution.

Then, of course, there are those more decisive instances of the making of America as recorded through its objects: those lanterns that illuminated the abolition marches; the silver-smithing of Paul Revere. Revere is mentioned only fleetingly in *A Useful Art*, as the probable master to apprentice silver-smith Zacharia Stevens, but in the combination of his craft and his sense of mercantile independence, Revere is integrally related to Zukofsky's "objective" American history.

As for the things, the design objects themselves, Zukofsky's treatment of them is such that his essays and scripts frequently fall into poetry, or at least, into his poetry. Primary to this is the detail of his descriptions. In section 8 of his major poem "A", Zukofsky writes,

> If you know all the qualities of a thing
> You know the thing itself;
> Nothing remains but the fact
> The said thing exists without us;
> And when your senses have taught you that fact,
> You have grasped the last remnant of the thing itself.

Zukofsky's day-job, in other words, researching, describing, was entirely of a piece with his vocation. Likewise, in his vocation it is arguable that Zukofsky considered himself in the tradition of the designers whose work he so admired, and not least in their way of presenting themselves. Thus, as *A Useful Art* tells us,

> The majority of craftsmen and their masters left no personal record. The ironwork and the industry they established tell the story of most of them. Occasionally their names were engraved or stamped on as object, most offered only their initials.

Whatever else "Objectivism" stood for, and it is a notoriously difficult term to get hold of, it indicated a determination on the part of its practitioners to get out of the way, to let the materials through.

Personally I would recommend *A Useful Art* to anybody who wants a way into Zukofsky's poetry, and into "A" in particular: a poem which is, no doubt, longer than it might have been, but which in the unceasing accuracy of its music is a great pleasure to spend time with. I would recommend it also to anybody who has always wanted to know – the clatter of kettles, and pots and pans notwithstanding – why "so much depends / upon // a red wheel / barrow // glazed with rain / water // beside the white // chickens". Mostly, though, I would recommend *A Useful Art* because it is a work of enthusiasm, and the world needs works of enthusiasm.

DAVID HERD

Poet in the Gallery

JEREMY OVER

Boyle Family
14 August – 9 November 2003
Scottish National Gallery of Modern Art, Edinburgh

You must love the crust of the earth on which you dwell more than the sweet crust of any bread or cake. You must be able to extract nutriment out of a sand-heap. You must have so good an appetite as this, else you will live in vain.

(Thoreau)

Thoreau would probably have approved of the Boyle Family, whose love for the crust of the earth and insatiable appetite for making art about it is comprehensively chronicled in this Edinburgh retrospective.

The project began forty years ago on a West London demolition site where Mark Boyle and his partner Joan Hills came across a discarded TV frame. The accidental "composition" within it, of various bits of building rubble, seemed beautiful to them. They tried several times to reproduce the effect themselves by deliberately moving the frame and choosing the contents of their own compositions. But it was only when they re-introduced the original element of randomness by simply throwing the frame up in the air and seeing where it landed that they liked what they saw again.

From that point on these two artists, alongside their children Sebastian and Georgia, who over the last twenty years have also worked with them, all exhibiting together under the name "Boyle Family", have dedicated themselves to reproducing incredibly realistic facsimiles of randomly chosen portions of the surface of the earth.

The roots of the Boyles' art lie in the '60s performance art and music scene, a fact that's hard to miss in the first rooms of the exhibition, which are devoted to their early junk assemblages and gloopy lava lamp light shows for Jimi Hendrix and Soft Machine (the first of their kind). There's also documentation relating to some of their "Happenings" such as "In Memory of Big Ed" which featured a staged interruption of a conference on the Theatre of the Absurd by a bagpiper and a naked woman wheeled around in a shopping trolley. And then there's "Graziella Martinez, the avant-garde dancer, performing on a tricycle with a growing projected scribble drawing". This is all a fairly good humoured exploration, I suppose, of the narrowing gap at that time between art and life, performer and audience (as well as a testament to what those audiences were prepared to put up with), but it does seem a bit of a sideshow to the Boyles' main work which since 1969 has been the "World Series" of earth presentations.

The sites for these works were chosen using a bizarre method that could have been devised by Raymond Roussel or Glen Baxter. Various people were invited to the ICA, blindfolded and then asked to shoot 1,000 darts at a 13'x13' map of the world. The Boyles committed to visiting each of the places that the darts had landed on to make an artwork. The precise selection process involves repeating the dart-firing at increasingly large-scale maps until the sites are of a suitably small size. When the family arrives there, one of them throws a right angle up in the air and where it lands determines the rectangle of the earth which is to be recreated in painstaking detail. The precise recipe for the mixture of media and methods used to do this is still a closely guarded family secret, but essentially it seems to involve part collage of some debris from the site – dust, sand, the odd twig or wire – and part creation of a painted fibreglass relief.

The mission to visit all 1,000 sites has some significant obstacles in its way. The Boyles still haven't conquered the technical difficulties of reproducing the surface of the sea, where two thirds of the darts landed. Also, the length of the whole process means that only some forty works have been completed so far. At this rate, finishing just the land-based part of the venture will take several generations; which, as there's no news of further little Boyles beyond Sebastian and Georgia at present, is a bit worrying. The project is in safe hands for the present though. A video in the exhibition chronicles a trip the family made to the Scottish Island of Barra to try and make one of their works. Stoical and determined, if a bit joyless in the wind and drizzle, it all seemed a rather typically British family seaside affair right down to the preoccupation with what was underfoot on the beach. Both daughter and father hint in the film at what they might have missed out on, as individuals and as a family, because of the obsessive nature of their art, but ultimately there is no real questioning of what they are here, on this earth, to do, which, according to Mark Boyle, is "to see without motive and without reminiscence this cliff, this street, this roof, this field, this rock, this earth".

The elaborate lengths the Boyles go to, to try and ensure the randomness of the selection of sites for their works and the superrealism of the finished objects, are attempts to remove all human traces of subjectivity, conditioning, and aesthetic prejudice; to see the world as if for the first time and then to present it to us for our similarly "motiveless appraisal". This phrase may sound rather dry but the Boyles are passionate about it. Religious even – there do seem possible analogies to Krishnamurti's description of meditation as the "choiceless awareness" of reality. Seeing the world with an "innocent" eye is itself a myth, of course, and the Boyles know this. I don't think they're seeking to persuade us to take up permanent residence in the wood that Alice visits in *Through the Looking Glass*, where things have no names. But they do seem to be making a strong case for seeing, if not with innocent eyes, then with wider eyes at least; for being more frequently and profoundly gobsmacked before the world.

It's a recurring aim of art to defamiliarize, to present the strange and extraordinary in the ordinary. The particular way in which the Boyles set about achieving this is by finding something, taking it out of its original context, and re-framing it within the gallery; also by carrying out a shift in planes from the horizontal earth to the vertical gallery wall. In the case of "Concrete Steps Study", in which steps are displayed flat against the wall like a sheet of corrugated iron, the effect of this shift is vertiginous. On the whole, though, this sort of de-familiarization technique is pretty familiar to us now. We are all becoming used to the idea of "found" objects in the gallery – urinals, sharks, unmade beds, light switches – but the Boyles do more than just find things.

I think the real reason why their work is so successful, why people stand and gawp at it in wonder, lies in the fact that it is made; made with great care and considerable technical sophistication. These objects are not just lumps of reality, but masterpieces of *trompe l'oeil*. I was suspicious of this at first. If the point is simply to present the earth to the viewer why not just photograph it, or actually bring the thing itself into the gallery and be done with it? Why go to these extraordinary and secretive lengths to make an artificial duplicate of the thing? I was also a bit embarrassed to find myself falling, along with all the others writing "How do they do it?" in the comments book, for what I felt was the work's superficial "Madame Tussauds" appeal. But I found that appeal lasting well after I'd finished staring at the last work in the exhibition, a flawless square of grass meadow ("Grass Study 2003") which seemed to pull everyone magnetically in to a distance of about six inches to inspect it.

It lasted until after I'd left the exhibition, spilling over into my walk back to the station along the freshly-made-grubby pavements of Edinburgh, past the little black splats of chewing gum, the golden yellow lines and sudden manhole covers, the carefully arranged leaves, cigarette butts, and litter with suggestions such as "eat, relax, linger". I found myself still looking and wondering "How do they do it?".

I don't know; and the Boyles, like genuine magicians, aren't telling. And I'm grateful to them for that. Because the artifice and the secrecy are vital, I think. They're what cause the curiosity, the staring in disbelief, the sniffing and the surreptitious prod (also frequently confessed to in the visitors book). Perhaps this is closer to "suspicious" than "motiveless" appraisal, but the end result seems to be wonder, whichever route you take. George Perec, in his essay "Approaches to What", recommends something like this investigative approach to what he called the infra-ordinary – that which usually goes without saying or seeing:

> What we need to question is bricks, concrete, glass, our table manners, our utensils, our tools, the way we spend our time, our rhythms. To question that which seems to have ceased forever to astonish us.

✐

Artists' Notes

This issue of *Poetry Review* launches Fred Mann's curatorship of the art pages. Eight pages have been allocated to include three artists per issue. In each issue, two of these pages will be devoted to an exhibition at the Whitechapel Art Gallery, London.

The Whitechapel pages in this issue show images from Franz West's recent exhibition *Franzwestite*. The Whitechapel exhibition scans the career of this seminal Austrian artist. In a playful critique of consumer culture, he paints over advertisements to isolate images, and to highlight their absurdity.

The pages devoted to the artist Cerith Wyn Evans show work exhibited at this year's Venice Biennale. Wyn Evans often takes poetry and converts key phrases into light, semaphore, mirrors, and exploded and unexploded fireworks. Shown here are two pieces quoting Gertrude Stein's "Before the Flowers of Friendship Faded Friendship Faded" (as unexploded fireworks, and as a mobile) and two pieces quoting the work of Pier Paolo Pasolini (as fireworks, and as morse code projected by laser).

Roger Hiorns has recently installed the work "Vauxhall" in the forecourt of Tate Britain. Oracle-like, a singular jet of fire rises from a metal grate set into the pavement. In the sculpture "Intelligence And Sacrifice", Hiorns uses milled steel, stainless steel, nylon, thistles, and copper sulphate to look at the nature of crystallisation and transformation. His third image here re-works an advertising image taken from a recent series exploring how images of youth are used to sell products.

For the Whitechapel pages, thanks are due to Iwona Blazwick, Frances Williams, Anthony Spira and Andrea Tarsia. Cerith Wyn Evans appears courtesy of Jay Jopling/White Cube, with thanks to Honey Luard. Roger Hiorns appears courtesy of Corvi-Mora, with thanks to Tommaso Corvi-Mora. Fred Mann is a director of Rhodes + Mann gallery London.

Letters to the Editors

MY THANKS TO Toby Litt, for coming at reading from self-observation, not from theory. Honestly watching what occurs – what ulterior motives and distractions we're apt to bring to reading poetry – would probably reveal that styles of reading are many and different and valid for different ends – in fact, incorrigibly plural. I don't think he need accept the academic test that reading *well* is reading to *remember*, that anything else is "failure". Most books I read, like most experiences and encounters, pass through me, and aren't fixed in memory . . . but I'm changed by them somehow – maybe more subtly so because it's been unconscious. I think of good advice I recently heard Helen Dunmore give historical novelists: do masses of research . . . and then forget it. It's that particular writerly sense of "forget" that we shouldn't forget.

Thanks too for naming the danger of being a member of the poetry business, as writer or as critic: over-consciousness. Apart from anything else, it's repellent to non-specialist readers (and if the majority of poetry readers aren't non-specialists then we aren't an art form, we're a cult). Let's remember what the sports bore sounds like – the study of form, the statistics, name-dropping and jargon – to those of us who sometimes like a good game. Or think how a good meal could be spoiled by dining with a dietician and a chef de cuisine.

The closing lines of Toby's article hint at the least likeable trait of the poetry world – the rivalrous reading, in reviews especially: reading to see off a threat or to establish dominance / deference / tactical alliance in the pack. In the same breath he suggests an ideal I'd pledge myself to work for: "reading without anxiety, without aggressively misreading" – without a peevish desire to put the writer in their place, or to remind ourselves of our own good qualities – reading generously, with a will to meet the writer's work as it is, aware of our own partialities, inviting a relationship that will develop over time. As writers, this means reading to be intrigued and unsettled as well as pleased, to spot new possibilities – keen, in fact, to learn. (After ten years of working on a Creative Writing Masters programme, I'm sure what teaches us to write is reading well.) I hope Mario Petrucci (Letter, vol. 93/2) is wrong in fearing that recent discussion of reading is all about inducting people into esoteric games. Anyone who has attended a poetry event hosted by Mario knows that generous acknowledgement based on accurate attention is what he does, and that's the style of reading we need, for the health of poetry.

Philip Gross

I THOUGHT THE latest *Poetry Review* was the best yet; the poetry in this issue was as interesting as the essays; in particular, the selection from Jane Griffiths, a name new to me, had what I look for in poetry yet rarely find: they were composed, yet startling.

The essay from Toby Litt was thought-provoking, though I wish he'd spent more time on reading poetry, since that was where he was at his best. It took me to back to Yeats – or rather, took me to Yeats for the first time, because, although I know certain poems quite well, I've not really "got round to him". It's good to have letters, as well, though the either/or (difficult/easy poetry) distinction of Mario Petrucci is a little tired. If Billy Collins, Jackie Kay and Henry Shukman are a good thing, it's because they're good, not because they're accessible. I would like to think I could give Ashbery's *Chinese Whispers* or Hill's *Speech! Speech!* to that same "anyone" and they'd be able to read it all the way through. I do feel that the great failing of our more accessible poets is how little they develop, how rarely they get "better".

Adrian Slatcher

———————————————

IT IS EASY to be at variance with Alex Smith's view (Letter, vol. 93/2), especially with reference to the "old" *Poetry Review* which was "simply a mishmash". He goes on to say, "This is not to knock the work of Peter Forbes". Er, actually, it is. The magazine had much to commend it. Not all mainstream publications which espouse a common-sense approach to poetry "play for safety". Even if they did, is a little conservatism such a bad thing?

One must admire and, to some extent, applaud the risk-taking of the new *Poetry Review*. It certainly has about it a breath of fresh air. The danger might be that this is too bracing for some, and that the chill draughts of avant-gardism now whistling under the door might alienate more readers than it wins. As with all experimentation, mistakes will occasionally be made. Messieurs Herd and Potts undoubtedly have enough wit to realise that catholicity of tone will satisfy the largest audience.

Paul Groves

———————————————

IT HAS BEEN drawn to my attention that a recent article in *Poetry Review* by John Wilkinson on Douglas Oliver states that the Allardyce, Barnett, Publishers collected edition of the late poet's work *Kind* is unavailable. That is not true. The cloth edition (which comprises work not available in other Olivier books) is in print and appears in our online catalogue at www.abar.net/litcat.html

Anthony Barnett

The *Poetry Review* Crossword

The sender of the first correct solution opened on 1 December will receive a cash prize of £20. Entries should be addressed to *Poetry Review* Crossword, 22 Betterton Street, London WC2H 9BX.

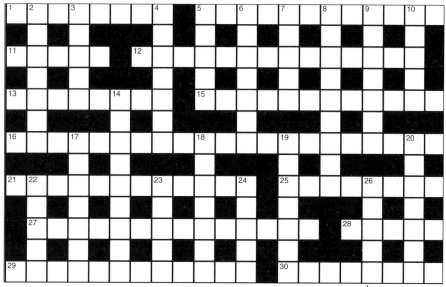

set by ANDRONYMOUS

Across

1 Editors spike the first piece (8)
5 Salon's crisis ruins cutting tools (12)
11 Subtle zebra holds back chisel tip (5)
12 Creamy sauce lies where 27's notes point (7,7)
13 Not yet parental, silly (8)
15 Long poem includes most English laws; note brief, witty style (12)
16, 21 From several points of view, 27's odd new ornithology is tat, a fake. Crow? (8,4,2,7,2,1,9)
25 27 wrote more than one article, each called First Love (8)
27 Poet calculated odds of Whitman eating shoestrings – good ones! (7,7)
28 Leave ring in game ring (5)
29 Scruffy topsheet, for example, demeans it, removes attraction (12)
30 Makes capital, which opens underwear (5,3)

Down

2 Intensifies what Bishop villanelle ends with (2,5)
3 "A mug is a mug is a mug is a mug"... (5)
4 Beat 50 in mound (7)
5 Viking destroys sleeping drone (5)
6 One morning, cheap writer begins to sing – de DUM, de DUM, de DUM (7)
7 Fears dispelled (5)
8 Inconvenience in convenience (9)
9 Remove top layer, as element protects the face (3,4)
10 Drain makes James a debunker of psychics (5)
14 Second thoughts at that time, and another time (4,5)
17 Polish the Spanish and the French bug (7)
18 A top-notch vest; undone flies (7)
19 Draws attention to understated relatives (7)
20 Chemical compound can draw up lift (7)
22 Break sweat on top whip (5)
23 Grovelled for grand (after tax) with lump-fish head in (5)
24 Birds plunged underwater over first setback (5)
26 Do badly but be sceptical (5)

Contributors

Paul Batchelor's chapbook *Fighting in the Captain's Tower* was published by Hawthorn Press. He received an Eric Gregory Award this year.

Simon Barraclough is a freelance writer currently living in London.

A. C. Bevan's first collection was *Of Sea-Graves & Sand-Shrines* (Arc, 2001).

Stewart Brown's most recent collection is *Elsewhere: New and Selected Poems* (2000).

Anthony Caleshu is Lecturer in Creative Writing at the University of Plymouth.

Linda Chase's latest collection is *The Wedding Spy*, published by Carcanet 2001.

Kate Clanchy's *Newborn* will be published by Picador next March.

Andrew Duncan's new collection is *Surveillance and Compliance.*

Carrie Etter is a Visiting Lecturer in Literature at the University of Hertfordshire.

Brian Fewster's first pamphlet collection was *Poor Tom's Revenge* (2002).

Yvonne Green's poems have appeared in various magazines and on *The Food Programme.*

Hamish Ironside is working towards the completion of a first book of poems.

David Kinloch's most recent collection is *Un Tour D'Ecosse* (Carcanet, 2001).

Richard Lambert lives in Bristol and has had poems published in various magazines.

Angela Leighton's last volume of poems was *A Cold Spell* (Shoestring, 2000).

Toby Litt's most recent novel, *Finding Myself*, is published by Hamish Hamilton.

Tony Lopez's latest collection is *False Memory* (Salt, 2003).

Sara Lundquist is an associate professor of English at the University of Toledo, Ohio.

Patrick McGuinness's translation of Mallarmé's *For Anatole's Tomb* was published by Carcanet this year.

E. A. Markham's *John Lewis & Co* (Anvil) was published earlier this year.

Janet Montefiore is Reader in English at the University of Kent.

Jeremy Over's *A Little Bit of Bread and No Cheese*, was published by Carcanet in 2001.

Mario Petrucci is a physicist and the Imperial War Museum's first ever resident poet. "Breathing", a revised version of his winning entry for the 2002 *Daily Telegraph / Arvon Competition*, is to be published in *Heavy Water* (Enitharmon, April 2004).

Richard Price's elliptical novel *A Boy in Summer* was published by 11:9 in 2002.

Jeremy Reed's new collection, *Duck and Sally Inside*, will appear next year.

Michael Symmons Roberts's fourth collection, *Corpus*, is published next August.

Fiona Sampson edits *Orient Express*. Her latest collection is *Folding the Real*.

Andrew Sant's *Selected Poems* will be published by Arc. He is the 2003–4 Writing Fellow at the Universiy of Leicester.

Simon Smith's latest book is *Reverdy Road* (Salt Publishing, 2003).

Robert Stein has published poems in a number of magazines including *Poetry Review, The Rialto, Envoi, Orbis* and *The Express.*

Dawn Wood lectures at the University of Abertay, Dundee, where she is writing a PhD on "The Poetry of Animal Husbandry".

Jonathan Treitel's poems have appeared in *Poetry Review, Ambit, London Magazine, Jewish Quarterly* and *Jerusalem Review.*

Jane Yeh's poetry pamphlet, *Teen Spies*, is available from Metre Editions.